SURRENDER

A BLACK MOTHER'S
CRY *for* HEALING *in*
a HEARTSICK WORLD

JULIA JACKSON

Copyright © 2023 by Julia Jackson
First Paperback Edition

All rights reserved. No part of this publication may be reproduced, distributed, or transmitted in any form or by any means, including photocopying, recording, or other electronic or mechanical methods, without the prior written permission of the publisher, except in the case of brief quotations embodied in critical reviews and certain other noncommercial uses permitted by copyright law. For permission requests, write to the publisher, addressed "Attention: Permissions Coordinator," at the address below.

Some names, businesses, places, events, locales, incidents, and identifying details inside this book have been changed to protect the privacy of individuals.

Bible versions used:

The Holy Bible, English Standard Version. ESV® Text Edition: 2016. Copyright © 2001 by Crossway Bibles, a publishing ministry of Good News Publishers.

Holy Bible, New International Version®, NIV® Copyright ©1973, 1978, 1984, 2011 by Biblica, Inc.® Used by permission. All rights reserved worldwide.

King James Version (KJV). Public Domain

Holy Bible, New International Version®, NIV® Copyright ©1973, 1978, 1984, 2011 by Biblica, Inc.® Used by permission. All rights reserved worldwide.

Written by Christen M. Jeschke

Published by Freiling Agency, LLC.

P.O. Box 1264
Warrenton, VA 20188

www.FreilingAgency.com

PB ISBN: 979-8-9888007-0-5
eBook ISBN: 979-8-9888007-1-2

Printed in the United States of America

Dedication

To my mother, Janie Carson Johnson. Mom, I can't put into words my gratitude for you. You've shared with me the stories of pain and suffering you endured even from a young age, yet despite it all, you choose to act with tender-heartedness. Instead of passing on a legacy of hurt, you abundantly gave love and comfort to anyone who needed it. You showed me how to love and how to forgive and forget. Once you learned about the love of Christ, you shared it with me and supported me on my journey from that point forward. I thank you from the bottom of my heart. I am so grateful that God chose you to be my mother. May the Lord bless you and keep you always.

Contents

Acknowledgments vii

Prologue xiii

1 Heart Change 3

2 A Different Way 15

3 Root Renewal 27

4 Death to Life 41

5 An Issue of Blood 53

6 Pain Has a Purpose 63

7 Love Your Children Before You
   Have Them 75

8 Hearts That Heal 85

9 A Humbled Heart 97

10 A Love without Fear 109

Epilogue: Full Surrender 119

Acknowledgments

My daughter Letetra, my firstborn baby girl. You are a gift from God given to a mom who was just a child herself, not knowing how we would make it. The Lord saw us through it all. I'm grateful for your life. And I pray in the name of Jesus that all your wisdom, knowledge, and strength will be used for the kingdom of God. I pray that you seek God and know him on a level that you never have before. God bless you. May God keep you, shine His light upon you, and give you His peace. I love you.

For my son Jacob, the Lord has shown you His power and His might. He has shown you His grace and mercy when you should have been dead three years ago—three years ago, He kept you here. He saved you for a great and mighty work in Him through Him and by Him. I pray that you have a heart of surrender that will be beyond your understanding and expectations. I pray you use your second chance for God's glory in every area of your life. I'm grateful for your life. I'm grateful for you, and I love you—blessings upon blessings upon blessings.

Megan, my baby girl, you have such a strong power in you. You have wisdom and discernment, love and peacekeeping, and you are a beautiful woman who is very precious, and deserving of the best of all things. I'm so grateful for your life, love,and just having you for my daughter has been a blessing!. I'm so grateful for you. Keep pushing towards that mark. Continue to let the Lord be your chief cornerstone because He is the Chief Cornerstone. I pray that you will open up, let the Lord take over, and have His way with you. In the name of Jesus, I love you.

Pauly, I am very proud of the man that you have become. We've had a lot of gaps in our relationship, but you can never tell that when we're together. I pray you'll open your heart to the Lord and His ways. Keep Him as the foundation of all you do—and Edifye. You will be more successful than you ever imagined with the Lord Jesus Christ. I love you beyond measure.

My beautiful Zietha, there's nothing like God's love and presence in times of pain and sorrow. If we look to Jesus, He can fill all those empty places like no other. Let your beauty glorify the Lord in every way. When you look in the mirror, you see a beautiful face. When you look into the Word of God, you will find a beautiful love letter—a love letter that is calling you nearer and closer to Him. In Jesus's name, I pray you will seek His presence and love and surrender your heart to Him. Love you, and be blessed.

Pastor James and Pastor Sharon Ward. Having pastors who teach and live the Word of God is a blessing. Thank you for always teaching the uncut,

Acknowledgments

unwatered-down Word of God. Thank you for all your prayers over the years and for being the best example of what a woman and man of God looks like. The leadership you have given me and all of us at Insight Church is full of the Holy Spirit and always led by the Holy Spirit. I'm grateful for both of you. I pray that the Lord will always keep you and strengthen you and lead you and guide you in all of your ways.

Christen and Tom, my publishers, editors, and writers. I'm so grateful for you, and thank you for tolerating me through this whole process. Thank you for your prayers. Thank you for being led by the Holy Spirit. I'm forever grateful to you and look forward to a long-standing relationship with you all. Blessings to you.

To the intercessory prayer team at Insight Church, Skokie, your support and prayers have kept me through this time for the last three years. And even the prayers you were praying before the incident in August of 2020, I'm so grateful for your love, support, and kind words. I'm grateful for you all. There are simply no words that can express how much you guys have helped me. I love you beyond measure. God bless.

Pastor Michael and Carol Curry—the first two pastors I was officially under the umbrella of at the beginning of my walk. Thank you for the love and encouragement you gave me so early on in my walk of faith. Thank you also for your support throughout the last three years. I remember a time when I was not going to come back to church. I got a letter from you. I don't remember the words in that letter, but it was so powerful that it gave me the strength to know that no matter what, I should still keep pushing and never give up. I appreciate you beyond measure. Blessings to both of you.

For my great aunt Nannie Grace Brooks Bruster, who is now with the King of Glory, I'm grateful for all your phone calls, prayers, conversations, and love. I miss talking to you all the time. And also to my late aunt, Mattie Lee Dean. I miss our talks. I miss our laughing. I'm so grateful for all of your support through this time, the last three years. Even though you've gone home to glory, I'll never forget how, no matter what was going on with you, you always picked up the phone to call and check on your little niece. I'm so grateful for your life. And I look forward to seeing you in Glory when it's my turn.

To all of my dear friends who have supported me, including Eileen Sullivan, Julie Harris, Wenda Smith, and Karen Sydney, I love you all so very much. I appreciate you being there to listen to me cry, to pray for me, to listen to my venting, and to uphold and support me. I pray that you all will come to the saving knowledge of Christ like never before. I love you all very much.

Acknowledgments

For everyone—and I do mean everyone who has been praying for my family and who has supported us in any way. Thank you. The Lord says that He blesses us to be a blessing. And when we bless others, He will bless us that much more. I thank you that you have carried my burden for me in prayer. Thank you for your love. Thank you for your support. I pray that you are blessed beyond measure and that the Holy Spirit will rain upon you and your families to prosper, protect, support, and provide for you with every spiritual blessing, in Jesus' name.

A special thanks to Elder Keith and his wife, Nicolette, for your support. Thank you to Elders Karen and Carlton Evans and Paula and Clarence Williams (Uncle Honey). Special thanks also to Chris and Marlin Lorenz. All of you have supported me on many different levels over the last ten years during my time at Insight church; I'm grateful for you. I love you, and God bless you.

"Two broken people will never be whole without Jesus."

Prologue

"The police shot Jacob ten times in the back!" I was shocked awake by someone screaming into the phone, words that I couldn't make out—chaos and pain.

Startled out of the deep sleep of a late afternoon nap, I couldn't fully grasp what I was hearing. The phone in my hand identified the caller as Laquisha, the mother of my son Jacob's children in Wisconsin. I was so tired that I almost ignored the call, never expecting the news she would relay.

"Laquisha, what are you saying? What are you talking about? I just talked to Jacob a little while ago, and he was fine."

My brain was still foggy from sleep, and Laquisha wasn't making any sense. I heard crying, screaming—more crying. I searched my muddled thoughts for any detail I knew to make sense of what I was hearing.

My son Jacob had called me earlier that afternoon. I chatted with him and his son Izrael as they walked through Walmart, excitedly buying supplies for Izrael's birthday party that day. They sounded happy and energetic as they enthusiastically chattered while walking through the store.

Jacob told me, "Mom, I was going to come to Evanston to celebrate Izrael's birthday with all of you, but Laquisha wanted me to barbecue, so we're gonna stay home." Jacob had lived with Laquisha for a decade and was dedicated to being fully in his sons' lives as he keenly knew the hurt of growing up without a present father, and he didn't want his boys to experience the same thing.

I told him I understood and ended the call with a warm smile and plenty of love, telling Jacob, "Okay, sweetheart, I am going to take a nap."

Jacob replied lovingly, assuring me that he would call again, saying, "I'll call you when we get ready to cut the cake and say, 'Happy birthday.'"

Izrael was my grandson, and it was important for me to celebrate him. As the call ended, I briefly considered going to Kenosha, Wisconsin, to join them, where they all lived together. However, thinking all the details through gave me pause.

Unfortunately, the relationship between Laquisha and my son Jacob had been extremely taxing almost since the beginning. I recognized the toxic dynamic between them and encouraged them to avoid the constant interactions that eventually led to conflict. As a woman, I spoke to Laquisha and tried to persuade her to move on with her life. "Girl, when a man's mama tells you to run, you better listen."

Prologue

Laquisha would call me to complain about conflicts between her and Jacob. When I would respond by contacting them both to get things straightened out, she would respond, "We okay, Mama. Just pray for us." The Lord knows that I have been praying for them for many years.

As a mother, I tried convincing Jacob to move out of the household he shared with Laquisha and get his own place. I said, "Let your kids come and visit you in the summer months or on weekends." Jacob's dad had been mostly absent from his life, and he didn't want that for his children. "Get your own place where your kids can come see you without having to witness the bickering between you and Laquisha." Jacob didn't want to leave his boys. I encouraged both him and Laquisha to get involved in regular church attendance and to seek professional counseling. Many times, I counseled them to dissolve their relationship. Jacob's siblings encouraged this as well.

I wasn't speaking to them out of a place of perfection, but out of hard-won lessons I had learned from my own mistakes. As I matured in my faith and life experience, I realized that without God at the front and center, a relationship would not work. It is just opening the door for the enemy to enter and wreak havoc. When two broken people come together to try to exist as a couple, married or otherwise, all the fractured pieces clash until they have one big broken collection of messy shards. There is no wholeness in this; those two people rely on each other to heal a void in each other that only Jesus Christ can heal. Two broken people will never be whole without Jesus. Only He can heal their broken pieces and draw them together in unity.

Things were too toxic between Jacob and Laquisha to allow anyone to thrive, and this dynamic was harming everyone in the situation—not to mention providing an increased risk of dangerous domestic disputes and altercations occurring between them. They had been together for ten years and had three children together and five between them, so love must have been there. However, they were like oil and water. Their love came from a broken place and not a healthy one, so it was filled with fighting and strife. They needed a healing love that comes only from God. These thoughts drifted in and out of my consciousness as I fell into the deep sleep of my nap.

As I slept, the buzz of my phone alerted me to a text. I glanced at it and read, "Mom, I may need to come and stay with you." He relayed a disturbing incident involving Laquisha that was unfolding.

Oh, my Lord, I thought, *here we go.* I had been worried about something like this happening between the two of them, and sure enough, things were already starting to unravel. I put the phone down, and this time, I fell into a restless sleep, worried that later I would have to face the chaos of whatever destructive dynamic was occurring between them.

The thoughts of that conversation were pushed to the back of my mind when I received the hysterical call from Laquisha. "The police shot Jacob," she sobbed again.

Honestly, my first thought was one of anger at Laquisha. I didn't believe her and wrongly assumed she was trying to stir something up. As I slowly grasped the reality of what she was saying, my anger spread. The text from Jacob pushed its way forward in my mind, and I realized that I was mad at both of them. I was furious that Laquisha and Jacob kept fueling the toxic fire between them when they had no business being together in the first place.

My disappointment at both of them welled then ebbed as the horror of what was occurring fully dawned on me. My baby had been shot. I didn't know if Jacob was alive or dead.

When I hung up the phone with Laquisha, my knees hit the floor, and I cried out to the Lord, "No, Jesus. No. Don't let this be—not this way. Don't let Jacob die in his sin. Not this way, Lord." I hitched in a broken breath as I implored, "But let Your will be done. And whatever you do, save his soul."

As those words final words left my tongue, I was instantly covered in a calm that descended over me like a warm blanket. Instead of being enveloped in panic and fear, I was wrapped in supernatural peace and comfort.

> *Thy kingdom come, Thy will be done in earth, as it is in heaven. (Matthew 6:10 KJV).*

> "Hearts must change for healing to happen."

1

Heart Change

Jacob was still alive. *Breathe.* My baby was still alive. That is all that mattered to me. Laquisha had overestimated the number of times that Jacob had been shot, but the fact was, the situation was beyond dire. After I got the news of the shooting, I rushed to make arrangements to get to Jacob. *At which hospital is he being treated? Will he survive? Will I be able to hug him again?* My thoughts were on my son.

While I was worried about my boy, the world was already weighing in on the devastating event. Sides were being chosen, and narratives were being formed. Everyone suddenly seemed to be an expert in a situation that they knew nothing about. While these divisions sprung up, a unity of a different sort occurred. As the story spread, people started praying. Prayer warriors from my church and worldwide began pouring out prayer over the situation. I felt the strength of the Lord over me, and I know that it was a direct result of these faithful prayers.

The footage of the incident was uploaded and released almost instantly to YouTube and media outlets. The shooting of my brown-skinned son by a light-skinned cop became a trending story that splashed across the screens of hand-held devices everywhere. Everyone had an opinion and wanted to use my son as an excuse for either side of the argument.

Amidst this rapidly snowballing political and cultural upheaval, I felt that people desired to use me as a puppet, pushing me toward a platform I didn't want to take on. The world has its ways, its vision, and its perspective, but over the years, I have gained a different kind of sight. I have been gifted with a Kingdom perspective that is counter to everything surrounding me. As I have grown closer to the Lord, I see that His ways are much different from those of the world, and that the lens He shows us life through is not the dirty, corrupted lens that society presents to us.

When Jacob was shot, his father, "Big Jacob," pushed for legal representation by those who travel from incident to incident looking to capitalize on circumstances that fit their agenda. I had no such agenda. First, I was a child of God, and second, I was a mother who was deeply saddened by the events of that August day. I was a mom who loved her son yet also recognized the sinful nature of humanity.

With these thoughts in mind, I tried to decline when pushed to speak at a press conference that the entire world would view. I wanted to be caring for my son, not working through the process of finding words that would soothe others. I didn't want to be at the center of the fast-growing flames of controversy; I wanted people to react with love and calmness as they carefully considered the circumstances that took place.

My pastor and his wife, James and Sharon Ward, were the first call I made after finding out Jacob was shot, and they upheld me as we prepared for the press conference. They had supported me from the moment I gave them the news but had been cautious—they did not want to step in to the situation without invitation. Pastor James and Pastor Sharon did not want to add to my stress and were content to pray and support me from afar, but I asked them to come to be there with me. I requested their soothing spiritual presence, and they showed up, covering me in prayer, encouragement, truth, and wise counsel.

During this time, my daughters Letetra and Megan were also pillars of support for me, and so was my son-in-law Alton (Megan's husband). I initially wanted to watch the press conference from my hotel room or the truck, but I was told repeatedly that, as Jacob's mother, I had to be in front of the cameras and say something. The lawyers insisted, and my children and pastors persuaded me that I had to speak at the press conference.

What could I say? I was heartsick. My heart was aching for my son, grandsons, and everyone involved. When someone is shot, his life is never the same, and neither is the life of the person who did the shooting. Hurt is experienced on both sides. The different types of pain all spring from a sin-based root.

Rioting and conflict-filled marches had broken out all over the city of Kenosha, and that hurt my heart as well. The circumstances with my son didn't justify more violence and ruin.

Nearly thirty years prior, I had watched with horror as the rioting erupted in Los Angeles as the "City of Angels" became a demonic playground. A young black man, Rodney King, had been pulled over for an alleged traffic crime and resisting arrest. He was savagely beaten by four white police officers in a tragic event that was captured on camera. King survived the attack, yet it seemed justice was not served as three of the four officers were acquitted, and the jury failed to reach a verdict on the fourth. These verdicts and the surrounding outrage pushed social and racial tensions to the forefront of a community scarred by continued abuses of their humanity. Six days of riots did not bring healing or produce positive change—they produced more pain, hate, destruction, and death. Over two thousand people were injured in those riots, and sixty-three people were killed, representing sixty-three families whose loved ones were stripped from their lives.

Justice may not have been in the courtroom, but where was the justice for these lives lost? Sin multiplied sin.

The Rodney King rioting sickened me. The rioting only served to cause further breakdown. Matching violence with more violence did not nurture healing. Humanity needed a radical heart change.

Kenosha was under similar unrest as riots and destruction of property became rampant. Protesters claimed to be acting under outrage on my son's behalf, yet my son didn't want that, and neither did I. The destruction was pouring out a curse of pain on an already hurting community and nation. It was fanning flames of hate and violence that were spreading across the country as similar outpourings of anger sprang up. I understood the emotions behind these events but not the actions.

My whole life, I have been a resident in beautiful brown skin, and believe me, I know the trauma-filled history of our dark-skinned lineage. I understand the pain of the racial disparities in America throughout history. I know American history, good and bad. I get it. I know about the sin of slavery. I know about the Jim Crow laws, the lynchings, the KKK, the massacres of Black Wall Street, and all of these other horrific events that have happened to the brown community and other people of color in America. I know that these heartbreaking wounds on our history are horrible and have created a deep chasm in the souls and spirits of many, yet revenge is for the Lord. The destruction in these situations will never make things better. My mama would say, "Two wrongs don't make a right." The Bible is firm in its instructions not to return evil for evil. All the damage and destruction being caused in Jacob's name weighed heavily on my heart as I thought about the upcoming press conference.

Back in my hotel room, I prepared to face the press the only way I knew how: I prayed. I fell to my knees and threw my hands in the air. I said, "Okay, God. This is crazy. They want me to speak in front of all these cameras and people. You know me. I am not a public speaker, and I have stage fright. I don't have the words. You give me the words. Tell me what I need to say, and I will say it, but it has to come from You."

I still did not know what I was going to say until the moment that I said it. With cameras flashing and reporters jockeying for position, the peace of the Lord remained with me. I stood in a group filled with lawyers and people who had never known Jacob yet pushed themselves forward, claiming to be family. It was overwhelming, yet I remained held in a pocket of peace.

Immediately surrounding me were my family and pastors—those in Jacob's life who had helped me care for him as a single mom. My daughters, Letetra and Megan; my stepson, Pauly; my son-in-law, Alton; my sister; and a few other close family members joined me as the spotlight turned toward us. Jacob's father and his brother and Jacob's half-sister Zeitha, were nearby.

Pastors James and Sharon Ward stood by my side, pillars of strength amid challenge. Pastor James spoke with the Lord's strength and confidence as he called our nation back to God, emphasizing, "We have a sin problem and not just a skin problem." He prayed that hearts and lives would be changed and that the Holy Spirit would unify us.

Once at the podium, it took me a moment to collect myself before I could speak. I started off quiet and unsure, but when Pastor James put his hand on my shoulder, it was as if I felt the power of the Holy Spirit descending upon me as I spoke. There is something powerful about touching and agreeing, and I felt God's Spirit flowing through me and welling up as my voice rose in confidence, volume, and certainty. The Holy Spirit gave me these words:

> *My son has been fighting for his life, and we really just need prayers. As I was riding through here, through the city, I noticed a lot of damage. It doesn't reflect my son or my family. If Jacob knew what was going on as far as that goes, the violence and the destruction, he would be very unpleased, so I'm really asking and encouraging everyone in Wisconsin and abroad to take a moment and examine your hearts.*

Citizens, police officers, firemen, clergy, politicians, do Jacob justice on this level and examine your hearts. We need healing as I pray for my son's healing physically, emotionally, and spiritually. I also have been praying even before this for the healing of our country. God has placed each and every one of us in this country because he wanted us to be here. Clearly, you can see by now that I have beautiful brown skin, but take a look at your hand, and whatever shade it is, it is beautiful as well.

How dare we hate what we are. We are humans. God did not make one type of tree or flower or fish or horse or grass or rock—how dare you ask him to make one type of human that looks just like you. I'm not talking to just Caucasian people. I am talking to everyone—white, black, Japanese, Chinese, red, brown. No one is superior to the other—the only supreme being is God Himself. Please, let's begin to pray for healing for our nation. We in the United States have been united. Do you understand what's going to happen when we fall because a house that is against each other cannot stand?

To all of the police officers, I'm praying for you and your families. To all of the citizens, my black and brown sisters and brothers, I'm praying for you. I believe that you are an intelligent being just like the rest of us—everybody. Let's use our hearts, our love, and our intelligence to work together to show the rest of the world how humans are supposed to treat each other. America is great when we behave greatly. Thank you.

I didn't want to be at that press conference, but I was grateful that I could glorify God in what I said. Our nation was crying out for healing, yet the tears were wasted on the false idols of sinful ideals. Our hearts needed to turn to the one true Healer, Jesus Christ. I was thankful to be able to point to Him in that moment.

Sadly, as soon as I stepped away from the microphone, my words were reframed—repackaged in a way desired by culture instead of the call given by Christ. Humanity has tried to do things their way, and all that ever results from that is evil, hurt, division, and heartache. People cried out in protest over the shooting of my son, yet they seemed blind to the solution for a problem that had been birthed from sin. The answer to the world's pain is found in the One who willingly sacrificed His Son for us all. Hearts must change for healing to happen.

Repay no one evil for evil, but give thought to do what is honorable in the sight of all. If possible, so far as it depends on you, live peaceably with all. Beloved, never avenge yourselves, but leave it to the wrath of God, for it is written, "Vengeance is mine, I will repay, says the Lord." To the contrary, "If your enemy is hungry, feed him; if he is thirsty, give him something to drink; for by so doing you will heap burning coals on his head." Do not be overcome by evil, but overcome evil with good. (Romans 12:17–21 ESV)

> "God's way looks very different from the way of the world."

2

A Different Way

While talking heads on TV were expressing their views on the unfolding situation, I was huddled in a car in the hospital parking lot with my family. COVID restrictions were tight, and I was waiting for permission to see my son.

After the call with Laquisha, I was able to briefly talk on the phone to a sheriff who was securing the scene. Laquisha had been understandably hysterical and difficult to understand. I didn't believe her when she told me Jacob had been shot. "Don't say that. No, no. That's not true. Don't say that. Don't start with me—let me speak with the police officer."

I couldn't make sense of what Laquishia was saying, so she handed the phone to the sheriff, and I asked, "Do you know what happened?"

"No, I do not know," the sheriff said honestly. "I do not know what happened. I'm just here to secure this."

"Okay. Do you know if my son is dead or alive?" I asked.

"No, ma'am. I don't know. All I can say is that it is bad, really bad."

I took a deep breath and replied, "Okay." At that point, all that was on my mind was getting to my son.

After that call and a brief call to my church pastors, there was a whirlwind of activity to get to Jacob. My mind moved 100 miles per hour, yet I was still at peace in a supernatural calm. I needed to get to Jacob, but I wasn't sure that I should drive myself. I knew that Big Jacob, Jacob's father, had been in the area, so I called him. After a brief and fruitless discussion, he hung up on me. My next call was to Shane, Letetra's husband at the time. It took us a few hours to get on the road. Shane had to pick up Letetra, my younger daughter Megan, and me before we could make our way to Wisconsin. While I waited, I called my mom and told her the sobering news.

As we drove the two-hour-long trip from where I was living in Mount Prospect, Illinois, to Kenosha, Wisconsin, I pulled up the incident video on YouTube. It was horrifying to see footage of my son being shot playing across the internet. I imagine that most people could watch the footage with complete detachment, but I could not. This was my son. This was my baby, who I delighted in as I watched him grow from infancy to adulthood. I held, rocked, nourished, and tried my best to guide him as he became a man. Jacob was such a joyful child. Whenever he walked into a room, he brought smiles and laughter. Jacob made it his mission to make me laugh if I was having a bad day. He had a way of exuding joy and fun to all around him. The world would be much kinder if we saw everyone as someone else's child instead of labeling by the shame of their mistakes or by the color of their skin.

I watched the shooting footage on repeat as I tried to figure out for myself what happened. The world was already peddling its perspectives, but I wanted to view the situation from an unbiased view. The media seemed to be split into two sides—one declaring Jacob a criminal who needed to be shot; the other declaring him a flawless victim. The sad truth is that neither of these perspectives captured the reality of a complicated situation. Loving my son dearly didn't mean I didn't recognize his flaws or capacity for error. Respecting the police didn't mean that I lacked the understanding that they could abuse or misuse power. We live in a broken and weary world.

The tragic circumstances surrounding the death of Breonna Taylor and George Floyd were at the forefront of the minds of those in the brown community. As I watched the agonizing replay of the video in a self-imposed version of barbaric catharsis, I thought back to conversations that my son Jacob and I had regarding the circumstances surrounding the murder of George Floyd.

My childhood introduction to the police was through the "Officer Friendly" program. The Officer Friendly campaign helped to acquaint children with police and view them as a safe resource. I had not been raised to fear the police. In fact, I delighted in the school programs presenting Officer Friendly as we learned more about the role of the police and got to view with wonder their police vehicles, uniforms, and flashing lights. As I raised my children, I taught them to respect authority. Police were authority figures, and it was imperative that my children behaved with care and courtesy if the police ever confronted them.

As time went on, with the evolution of smartphones and the media attention on what was occurring between citizens and the police, it became harder for me to defend the police to my children. We saw stomach-churning injustices playing out right in front of us that undermined the lessons that Officer Friendly had taught me—that police officers are always good and are to be trusted. I felt as if my children were thinking, "Mommy, you lied to us." The fact is that I knew that anyone could make bad decisions, no matter the career choice or employment status, and that the police were not immune from making destructive decisions.

The reality was that, like many in the brown skin community, I worried for the protection of my children as well as my grandchildren. Although I didn't fear the police and I raised my children to respect them, this didn't mean they always behaved appropriately regarding authority. My girls were always straight-A students, but Jacob had a rebellious spirit, and I worried this could one day cause him trouble. I was especially nervous about him in this regard. His father had been absent from his life when Jacob was growing up, and I feared that the lack of a male role model would someday harm him.

"Jacob, if you ever get stopped by police, don't forget what to do," I cautioned.

"Oh, Mama, come on. You taught me. I know what to do," Jacob replied. "Plus, the police out here, they are cool. They don't do that. They don't just come up here and grab you. It is not like Chicago or something."

"Please just don't get too comfortable and familiar," I chided.

"Oh no, Mama, they listen. As many times as the police have been called on me and Laquisha, I would know. They listen. They don't just jump to conclusions."

"Just be careful," I reiterated more pointedly this time.

Following this directive, conversation resumed normally as we shared our private thoughts and feelings about the George Floyd situation. We both expressed what we thought the video showed. I made the observation that I thought Officer Chauvin had a bad spirit in him. The way that he looked at the camera with his hand in his pocket as George Floyd fought for life beneath his knee seemed demonic. I could see the darkness in his eyes as if he were consumed by an evil spirit bent on destruction.

Jacob replied to my pondering, "You know what, Mom? I think that you are right." Jacob agreed with me that there was something demonic about that entire situation.

This thought burrowed in my mind, floating to the surface as I watched the film of my son being shot seven times in the back. So many things were wrong in that situation. It was a domino effect of disaster that ended in the mutilation of my precious son's body. *What could have been done differently? Why couldn't Jacob come back to Evanston to celebrate? Why couldn't Laquisha just let him leave with the boys peacefully?* He would never hurt his sons. *Why did she have to call the cops? Why didn't Jacob stop when the police told him to? Why did he scuffle with them? Why didn't he respond to the Tasers? Why did he have a knife? Why didn't the officers try to work things out peaceably? Why couldn't they shoot his tires instead of his body? What could have been done differently?*

I watched the footage again and again, trying to seek out conclusive evidence for any one point of view, but I could not. I had so many questions but no solid answers. Everyone made bad decisions that day, but my son did not deserve to be shot seven times in the back. All I saw was my hurting son, who could lose his life due to the effects of a heartbreakingly sinful world.

At Froedtert Hospital, we were told that they had taken Jacob into surgery and that he couldn't have any visitors because he was under arrest. They told us that his arrest was allegedly for a warrant for rape. This was a shock to all of his family members, and it didn't seem that it could be real. It didn't seem in Jacob's character, so this allegation shook us all. (We did not believe this at all! And for me I know that if he had lost his mind and did that, Laquisha would have told me.) Due to COVID protocols and restrictions, we were told that we had to stay outside until instructed otherwise. Sheltered in the vehicle in the shadow of the looming hospital structure, we began an agonizing wait for news.

As we awaited updates on his condition, the world repeatedly watched the incident footage online. Letetra told me it was on YouTube when she called me frantically. Still, it hadn't registered to me that it was a viral moment forever memorialized on film and rapidly spreading across social media. The film of one of our worst days as a family was spreading fast on YouTube, Facebook, and Twitter. Everyone seemed to be watching and calling. My phone was going off like crazy as people called and texted, trying to find out anything that they could. Eventually, it became so overwhelming that my daughter Meghan gently placed her hand over mine and wisely removed the phone from my hand.

At that time, I was addicted to nicotine, and smoking was a habit for me. I took regular smoke breaks while we waited, yet not due to anxiety over the situation. My need to smoke was an addiction that stood in sharp contrast to the Holy Spirit's calm that I felt.

A local minister, Pastor Radontae Ashford from The Infinite Church in Milwaukee, Wisconsin, had seen the news of the shooting and figured that we might need support. He thought we might possibly be at the hospital nearby, so he searched the parking lot for us, and sure enough, there we were. He offered to pray for us, which was a rich encouragement and blessing to my family during that time. It was amazing that he would show up without knowing us, offering prayer and asking how he could help. Later, some other members of his congregation came and brought us water and juice. This church provided meals for at least twenty of us on multiple occasions. This was a beautiful gesture that brought a healing balm to our souls. The minister said that he had to come to pray with us and check on us. His actions were a faithful act of obedience to the Lord, which was magnified in its soothing effect on us.

Meanwhile, Pastor James, Pastor Sharon, and my church home congregation prayed for me from afar. I initially told them not to come because their prayers would be powerful, no matter where they prayed, and they agreed. The Wards had also just been traveling, and knowing how busy our pastors were with the needs of their flock, I didn't want to add to their commitments. I didn't want to burden them in any way. They waited in prayer until I invited them to come.

The hours ticked by slowly as we waited in the car for news of Jacob. By two or three in the morning, we realized that we needed to make arrangements for a hotel. My niece made the arrangements, placing the charges on her credit card, and we all chipped in, sending her money as reimbursement. A few days later, we discovered that people had donated to cover our costs and hotel stay. It seemed that amidst the darkness and unending challenges, there were glimmers of love, kindness, and light.

This love and outpouring of generosity starkly contrasted the occurrences surrounding us. God's way looks very different from the way of the world.

For this is the will of God, that by doing good you should put to silence the ignorance of foolish people. Live as people who are free, not using your freedom as a cover-up for evil, but living as servants of God. Honor everyone. Love the brotherhood. Fear God. Honor the emperor.. (1 Peter 2:15–17 ESV)

> ""It was better that he have a saved soul than an untorn body."

3

Root Renewal

Waiting to physically see Jacob was agonizing. I just wanted to see my son with my own eyes and know if he would be okay. When I finally saw Jacob in his hospital room, I felt as if I were walking through some sort of strange dream.

I gathered myself briefly in the hallway. I paused before entering Jacob's ICU room for the first time to take a moment to prepare myself. I knew he had already been through surgery, but for some reason, I expected to see him covered in blood with tubes and equipment attached to his body—*deep breath*. Amazingly, I still felt that supernatural sense of calm that had rested on me since the moment of my first prayer.

As I cautiously walked in, I made eye contact with the nurse caring for Jacob. She gave me a crooked smile before pulling back the curtain to reveal Jacob sitting in the bed, his head turned away from me. He heard me enter and slowly turned his face to see me. When he realized it was me, his head dropped nearly to his chest, and he sobbed, "I'm sorry, I'm sorry."

The dam of tears that held back the tumultuous waves of my emotions broke at that moment as I sobbed beside my son. This is every mother's worst nightmare. To lose or almost lose a child is an experience that no parent should ever go through. It was heartbreaking to see Jacob in the hospital. Heartbreak turned to hope with the reassurance that my boy was alive—I could wipe his tears, touch his skin, hear his voice, and know he would be okay. I cried heavily, feeling the weighted mixture of sadness and joy.

When Jacob was a baby, he cried all of the time. Many babies cry at birth, calling out a need to be nurtured and loved. Some babies cry from discomfort or maybe colic, but I often have wondered if there is more to an infant's cry. Some infants cry once they are removed from the protection of the womb as if they sense the weight of sin and sadness in the world surrounding them. They seem to know they will face challenges, trials, and tribulations. Maybe some babies cry more than others because they have the weight of a bigger destiny—I don't know, but I do know that Jacob cried a lot.

On one occasion, I took Jacob to see my grandmother in New York, and Jacob cried so much that he wore her out. I tried to soothe him by walking around a courtyard, rocking and bouncing him in my tired arms. He screamed louder. The surrounding neighbors poked their heads out the window to shout, "Shut that baby up." I can't say what my response was because, well, I hadn't surrendered at all back then. I can just say that it wasn't a kind response or thoughtful reaction. It was one that welled up from deep inside my sin-filled heart as I lashed out in anger.

Seeing my boy in that hospital bed, all shot to pieces, almost pulled me back to the place of that sinful pain-filled response. Jacob was a grown man but was also my baby, who I had carried for nine months. I had raised and nurtured him, bandaging scraped knees, praying away bad dreams, and comforting him when something hurt his little heart. I had tried my best to love, protect, and teach him to do what was right with the only knowledge I had at that time. I raised him from my own limited understanding without realizing that all along, I had held the manual right in my hand, the Word of God.

It was very hard to let go of pain and maybe even the right to cling to anger. Jacob's body had been tattered and torn, but he was still alive. He may never be the same physically, emotionally, or mentally, but his soul was saved. It was better that he have a saved soul than an untorn body.

I can't imagine how hard it must be for someone to lose a child under any circumstances. Whether it is a shooting, a natural death, a sickness, a disease, or something else, losing a child must be the most difficult thing for anyone to go through. But one thing I do know without a doubt is that no matter what the pain is, the Lord can heal us. The hard part is that we have to allow Him to do that. We have to expose our hurt and pain and ask for His healing.

At that moment in the hospital, a part of me wanted to cling to pain and let it feed hatred, but I had tried that in the past and knew that it only produced more pain. Instead, I knew I needed to ask God for healing and trust Him as He worked. This turned my heart toward prayer. I prayed for those who hurt us, for those who hated us, and also for those who showed love toward us and were reaching out in support. The Lord wants us to pray for all people, and as I did that, my heart began to view the entire situation with compassion and understanding instead of hate and rage.

The peace that surrounded me and the healing nature of prayer ministered to me, but it did not make me blind to the circumstances in front of me. Jacob had been shot seven times, twice in the arm and five times in the back, dropping the bullets into the abdomen.

One of the doctors treating him told me that after the injuries that Jacob had sustained, he shouldn't have been alive. He also stated that he had never seen anyone survive after the amount of damage that had been done to his body. Another doctor, an anesthesiologist, discussed Jacob's case with unusual excitement, proclaiming that he saw God at work. He was impacted almost to the point of tears, saying that he knew that God had saved Jacob, as there was no other explanation for how he could still be alive. He declared it miraculous.

Most of Jacob's small intestines and colon had to be removed, and there was damage to his stomach, kidneys, lungs, and liver. A part of his spine had also been severed, and he was paralyzed from the waist down. I knew Jacob's life would never be the same, but I was thankful he was alive. I rejoiced even as I mentally started calculating what we would need to do to care for him when he left the hospital.

A few months earlier, Jacob and my son-in-law at that time had helped me move into a new place. I had broken my foot two weeks earlier, and they were helping me to get situated. Tired from their labor, they told me, "Mom, you gotta get someone else to move you again. We are getting too old for this."

I told Jacob that I was going to stay there. "Until I can buy my own home or get married, I am going to stay here," I said. Then I laughed, "I'm never getting married again, so I guess I'll just be here."

As soon as they left, I heard the calm voice of the Holy Spirit say, "No, you are not going to live here long."

I thought of that word of knowledge as the days in the hospital stretched on, and it became clear that

Jacob would need full-time care. It seemed that God had been preparing my heart in advance for things that would come and the reality that I would need to move to care for him.

Jacob's time in the hospital seemed like some sort of strange dream to me. I watched events play out around me that I had no control over. I remember feeling irritated as more people arrived daily.

It didn't take long before people saw the news and began showing up at the hospital. At first, friends and family from Jacob's life that I was used to seeing came by, but then people I had never seen before started to appear. "Relatives" from Jacob's father's side came out of the woodwork. None of these people had been there for Jacob when he was growing up, yet suddenly they placed themselves in front of the media for interviews. "Family member" after "family member" gave media interviews on behalf of Jacob, yet they were not his family at all. The Blake family had been largely absent when Jacob was growing up. His father had not been very present in Jacob's life financially or otherwise as I was raising him. I felt that the Blake family was showing up too late. When I say late, I mean that they should have been there when he was growing up. Many times I needed help with Jacob when he was having troubles, but none of them were ever there, so I was angry with them.

To be completely honest, I was so angry with Jacob's father and the Blakes that I had to separate myself and pray really, really, really hard. It wasn't that I was angry so much at each individual, but I was angry at their behavior. They weren't showing up for Jacob, or they would have done that all along. They were showing up for their self-interest, which was evidenced in how they acted. They were using the situation with Jacob to gain media time or push an agenda, yet they didn't even know my son, his perspective, or his heart.

Amazingly, as I wrestled with God and my anger over that situation, I realized I was not angry toward the police officer. I am not saying that the officer didn't do wrong or shouldn't face discipline within the justice system. What I am saying is that, on some level, I understood it. Between COVID lockdowns and all the racial craziness occurring, an ongoing spiritual battle played out in front of our nation. A current was rising that divided us through hatred and unrest. I watched it play out in the media and the politics of our country until it reached a boiling point. For whatever reason, God allowed this tragedy to occur to my family, and I recognized that He must have chosen us for His purpose. My anger was less at the officer and more at the people who should have been there before this happened. Maybe if the Blakes had been there in a positive way during Jacob's formative years, he wouldn't have been shot that day, or perhaps he still would have. It is hard to know.

My feelings toward the officer were mostly questions that begged, *Why couldn't you have done things differently?* I watched the shooting footage on repeat to try to answer that question and others. What should Jacob have done or not done? How could the police have handled it differently? Why did Laquisha say what she said in the 911 call? It was a twisted triangle in which sin wreaked havoc.

Jacob, Laquisha, and the police—they all played an unfortunate role in what happened that day. Laquisha's fight with the neighbor and the misleading 911 call were responsible for the police being there that day. Jacob's response to the police and his behavior rest on his shoulders. The police were acting on information that they had, but instead of grabbing Jacob from behind and activating a fight or flight response, maybe they should have begun by calmly talking things through.

From Jacob's perspective, he thought that the police were there regarding the fight between Laquisha and her neighbor. He was trying to get his sons out of an escalating situation in his home. If he genuinely didn't know that the police were there for him and they suddenly grabbed him from behind, that was a problem. In dealing with anyone who has undergone any trauma, but particularly in heated domestic situations, wisdom has to be applied to try to maintain calm instead of inflaming already fiery emotions.

Should Jacob have stopped when the police told him to stop? Yes. He should have done what he was told. If the police do something wrong, I always told my children, we'll deal with that later, but you do what you are told. So Jacob should have stopped. Many people don't understand this because all they see are black and white, police officers, and racial discrimination. Nobody wants to ask, what did I do wrong? All I am saying is that many actions could have prevented this.

For instance, I will move away from Jacob's situation to Sandra Bland. She was pulled over, and the police asked her to put her cigarette out. She refused. What ensued after that was heartbreakingly tragic. *Why didn't she just do as she had been asked?* Stick with me here—I am not saying that Sandra brought this on herself. I am going somewhere with this direction of thinking.

Back when I used to smoke, one night after work, I got pulled over while I was smoking a cigarette. I put it out right away. The officer didn't even have to ask. Why? I offered because smoking is a terrible, nasty habit, and the officer didn't deserve to have smoke blown in his face. I cared about the officer's feelings. It doesn't matter whether it is a police officer asking you, someone begging on the street, or a family member that you love—it would be respectful to put the cigarette out. Do you see what I am saying? We have to change our way of thinking. We have to consider others as better than ourselves and act with love.

What if Sandra Bland had put out her cigarette? Would it have changed the outcome? What if George Floyd didn't fear the police, and they reacted with compassion? Would it have made a difference? What if the police officers had knocked on the door at Breonna Taylor's house and asked for everyone's ID before going in? Would that have stopped a tragedy? What if my son had stopped when he was told? Would that have prevented the shooting? What if laws were in place for better training and accountability for police officers? Would they have changed any of these circumstances? Sadly, I don't believe that they would have.

Our societal problem goes far beyond any solutions we can come up with—other than the cross of Christ. As long as sin and rebellion against God and His ways are in the world, and as long as we refuse to look at ourselves and our hearts as individuals, nothing will change. The killings are getting more frequent. On every level, this whole world is in shambles—every country, every city, and quite frankly, every neighborhood. Even perfectly manicured neighborhoods are hiding sin behind a more attractive façade. Changing the outside appearance never gets to the root. It doesn't make a difference.

The difference maker is when we can start abiding by the Word of God. Many people may not want to read it—maybe they don't believe it. Perhaps it's because the Bible says that the Word of God is alive, sharper than any two-edged sword, piercing the hearts of men. Maybe we don't want to read the Word of God because we don't want to have to look at ourselves. We don't want to be corrected. We don't want to be called sinners. Yet, if we say we're not sinners, we lie. And we're calling God a liar. But more and more, I'm learning the fear of God. I'm learning the compassion of Christ and how we, as believers, are supposed to reflect and or be ambassadors of Christ on the earth.

We don't know if the outcomes of those tragic situations could have been different. However, I do know that if our hearts are changed and renewed, everything will change. My heart is longing for others to experience this change even as I mourn not just the incident with Jacob but also the loss of two young family members recently to gun violence. It is devastating. My heart goes out to all the families who have lost loved ones from gun violence of any type. We have to get back to Christ. We have to get back to the Word to see a change.

We can't simply claim to be victims. We have to examine our sins in every situation and search our hearts for anything impure and wrong. Until we do this, our actions are those of hypocrites who claim to want restoration while seeking to cause division instead. I had to scour my heart for its own impurities as I fought to keep a godly perspective amid all that was occurring, and I continue to do so daily.

> *Submit yourselves therefore to God. Resist the devil, and he will flee from you. Draw near to God, and he will draw near to you. Cleanse your hands, you sinners, and purify your hearts, you double-minded. (James 4:7–8 ESV)*

"Every promise that God makes is true."

4

Death to Life

When I was seventeen years old, my mother got remarried. Initially, I did not like her husband at all. To say that I couldn't stand him was an understatement. We got off to a very rough start. However, as my mother and her husband began to go to church together, the frosty divide between her husband and me started to thaw. I started attending church with them, trying to understand through much skepticism what this "church stuff" was about.

At eighteen years old, I became pregnant with my first child. Scared and unsure of how life would turn out, I sought guidance from my mom. That night, a conversation with my mom and her husband turned into ministry as they shared wisdom and a hope-filled future. We talked about faith, Jesus, and salvation. They asked me if I wanted to accept Jesus Christ as my Lord and Savior. I responded, "Yes," and there in my mom's room, I asked Jesus into my heart. It was a simple decision made without fanfare or full understanding, but that act of faith gradually changed my life.

Several months later, my biological father passed away, and I attended his funeral in New York. After the funeral, I brought his Bible home with me. Unzipping the black leather case revealed pages of black typeset print on thin rice paper. It was a red-letter Bible, the words of Jesus neatly displayed in a red font. A heavy King James Version translation, I couldn't make heads or tails of the old-sounding language. I struggled to read many words because I wasn't good at it. The more I read, the more I realized that I couldn't make sense of what it was saying.

I became frustrated. I was trying to learn more about God, but the Bible seemed so complicated. Finally, I began praying—a conversation between God and me. I said matter-of-factly, "God … well, you know … I was told that Jesus Christ is the Son of God and that this book, the Holy Bible, is the living Word of God. So, God, if this is true and You want me to read it, give me the wisdom to read." Each time I tried to read the Bible but couldn't understand, I would pray this prayer.

This went on for a while—me trying to read the Bible, growing frustrated that I couldn't understand it, and then repeating some variation or another of that same prayer. Then, one day, I picked up the Bible, and it was as if someone had turned on a light in a dark room. Suddenly, I could read and understand in a way that had been impossible before. I became captivated by the Word of God. His Word was living and active, piercing my heart in a way I had never experienced before, ministering over me in peace, grace, and mercy.

My process of surrendering to God and allowing Him to lead my life took many years. I made more mistakes than I should have, and for far too long, I lived with one foot in the world and one in the church. I wanted to do things my own way and in my own understanding, but my way led to hurt and destruction over and over again. Learning to surrender was a hard-won lesson, but I am thankful for God's grace and mercy as I struggled through.

For many years, I deceived myself into thinking that my way was working. I thought I could be a Christian without fully surrendering my heart to God. The problem was that my continued sin and corrupt way of thinking were harming me. Sin was causing havoc and pain in my life that was increasing instead of decreasing. Each time I tried things my own way, I wandered farther from the path of good and righteousness that my heavenly Father had for me.

I had gotten into a relationship that was beyond toxic. It was a shameful, demonic relationship. It was broken and destructive and tore at everything that God made me to be. It covered me in spirits of sin that were trying to dismantle me. When I escaped that relationship, I repented and asked God to restore and cleanse me from that evil bond. God was faithful. He cleansed and delivered me from the torturous spirits of that defiling relationship.

After I recovered from that broken relationship, instead of abiding in the Lord, I pushed myself into yet another relationship with my high school sweetheart. Rekindling a flame that should have never been relit to begin with, I married him. I knew it was not a relationship from the Lord, but I did it anyway. I felt that I was getting old and didn't want to be alone. I grew up surrounded by a big family, and as my kids grew older, I worried about being by myself as they began to leave the nest of my home. I acknowledged that it wasn't what God wanted, yet I acted in disobedience. Disobedience is never without consequences.

This fear of being on my own had a spiritual solution. I could have brought it before God, knowing He would supply my need and gather community and support around me. He would have bolstered me in His Word and strength. However, instead of trusting in Him, I took things into my own hands. Knowing it would probably not work, I married my high school love.

I knew that I was longing for a love that only Christ could fill, yet I chose to fill it with a man instead of following the Lord's will for my life. My disobedience bore fruits of destruction, and as my marriage dissolved in 2013, I found myself totally bereft.

Coming home from work to the utter desolation of an empty house, I fell onto the kitchen floor and sobbed. I lay on the floor as tears flowed in rivulets down my face, pooling on the floor beneath me. I had married so I wouldn't be alone, yet somehow I ended up at the very place that I wanted to avoid. I felt broken beyond repair. I had pushed God away to pursue my own plans, and I felt ashamed of my failure and trapped in a place of darkness.

I had cried enough tears for a saltwater baptism, yet I still felt stuck in a deep depression. Though He felt far away, God had not given up on me. He pursued my heart and His promise for my life. It wasn't easy, but God gave me the strength to keep going to church. I joined Insight Church and went to their first service, and then began attending their second service as well. I pushed myself to go to Sunday service, no matter how I felt. I knew that I needed the presence of the Lord, and it was just as crucial to my survival as getting up every day to go to work or coaxing myself to take a bite of food here and there. Many days, I wanted to remain in that puddle of tears on the floor, but I knew that I had to keep going, and God was faithful in giving me strength.

Days of depression stretched into weeks and months until one day; I once again cried out to the Lord—the pain in my heart laid bare. My life felt like a waste of years and years of bad mistakes, heartache, and pain. I had tried to move forward in my own direction, but each wrong decision I made pulled me backward. I was tired of living this way and begged God to intervene.

As I pleaded with the Lord, He answered me. He told me to repent of my sins; the sins of my parents, my grandparents, and my entire family; and on behalf of our nation. I obeyed. I cried out in repentance. He then instructed me to repent before my children for not living in the way that a woman of God is supposed to live. I had to humble myself and repent for setting a bad example before them as to who Christ was. It was a sobering realization that my disobedience and lack of surrender to Christ had hurt not only myself but also my children. It had given them a distorted version of who God was instead of the clear truth of His Word. I repented and urged them to watch me going forward. I wanted them to follow me as I followed Jesus and allow themselves to follow Him too. That remains my hope.

During this process of repentance, God also brought me to a place where I didn't let society bother me anymore. The pain of social justice, a conflict in my job, or the politics of America were things that used to make me angry or upset. However, during this time, the Lord brought me to a place of peace where I learned how to pray for people instead of feeling hurt and unsettled. As my confidence in God grew, I knew I could pray and trust Him with these heavy burdens.

This surrender was nearly effortless for me to do on a larger scale, but I struggled more when applying it to my personal life. It was difficult to navigate the feelings of hardship and hurt from the people I was closest to. I wish that I could say that God has smoothed out all my rough places in that regard, but the truth is that I still struggle with it even as He works to refine me. He has brought me to a higher place, but I am still a work in progress.

For me, it is often easier to forgive strangers for the things that they have done than to forgive friends and family members. I think this is because when someone is close to me, I place an expectation of love and protection that I don't on strangers. If a stranger hurts me, I don't have an expectation either way, but if someone close to me wounds me, it feels like a deep betrayal. I wrestle with this a lot.

I definitely grappled with this in the scene that occurred with Jacob and the police officer. While I could quickly release what the officer did through the power of forgiveness, this was not so easy for me within the relational dynamics around me. The Bible tells us in Matthew 10:36, "And a person's enemies will be those of his own household." I really beat myself up over this. I let a lot of things that occurred at that time bother me. I struggled with bitterness and unforgiveness. It has been three years since the shooting, and I am still trying to work through my hardheartedness. When I focus on the pain and hurt, Satan can convince me to take my mind and eyes off Christ, and I know that is a recipe for destruction that will set me back again. So I can't do that. I have to forgive—not in my own strength, but in Christ's.

When I feel unforgiveness and resentment welling up, I know the enemy is attacking, and I am given a choice. I can give in to the enemy and feed the turmoil of my thoughts, or I can draw closer to God. When the enemy attacks me this way, I say, "Okay, Lord. I messed up again. I tried to fix things, but I forgot Your Word. I listened to other people's advice and words instead of standing on the Word of God. Please help me surrender to Your will and Your way." When I surrender my sins and stubbornness to Him, He is always faithful to forgive me and gently guide me back to where I should go.

I am learning, and I still find myself often praying this prayer or a similar one. Far too many times, I have listened to the advice and opinions of the world, and it has always failed me. Listening to God's Word takes discipline, but it never lets me down. God is with me wherever I go, and no matter what happens or what anyone else says, I must listen to His voice. God's mercy, His kindness, His correction, and His direction are awesome and mighty. I am grateful for the patience of an almighty Father who works on me daily to take me to a higher place of surrender in Him.

Years ago, when I opened that King James Bible and asked God to help me read and understand His Word, and He did, I was so profoundly blown away by the Holy Scriptures. After living a life of walking without the Word in contrast to now walking in accordance with it, I am even more astounded as I read now. It took me a long time to see that the Holy Bible is God's Word exactly as I had been told, but what amazed me even more was that God directly spoke to me through his Word. The Bible was His love letter to me. At first, in every way, this was difficult to acknowledge. It was hard for me to accept that the God of the entire universe, who had created all things, loved me. He loves me! The sinful wretch that I am, His love for me is complete, whole, unfailing, unconditional, and everlasting.

For me, this view of a loving heavenly Father was very difficult to realize fully. Although I had a Bible from my earthly father, I never really had a father figure in my life who resembled Christ. This was my issue growing up. I was always looking for the love that can come only from God. This love is supposed to be modeled by our fathers—our earthly fathers, representing God in their families. This is what was missing in my household as a child. This generational failure occurred again in my own household when I was raising my children. They weren't rebellious children per se—they just did not grow up with a male figure at all. They definitely didn't grow up with a male figure who resembled Christ. My children grew up in a way that was broken. I was part of this brokenness. I had raised my children as a broken woman who had faith yet believed that the Word of God wasn't for me personally. I wished that I had learned sooner that His Word was for me. This would have influenced my family powerfully.

God's living Word is true. Every promise that God makes is true. Jesus Christ was crucified and raised after three days from the grave. He conquered sin for us only by His blood. The beginning of the Bible tells the story of the first man created, a man named Adam. He was tempted and fell into sin and disobedience to God. Adam was a man with blood full of the sand of sin and shame. Jesus' death on the cross for our sins covered us in the blood of His righteousness. He gave up His life so that we can live eternally with Him. That is true, pure, sacrificial love—a love without sin or personal gain. When we accept Jesus into our hearts, we are adopted as sons and daughters of God. Through this, we are gifted a personal relationship with Christ and the blessing of the Holy Spirit living inside us and speaking to us through God's Word.

And we have the prophetic word more fully confirmed, to which you will do well to pay attention as to a lamp shining in a dark place, until the day dawns and the morning star rises in your hearts, knowing this first of all, that no prophecy of Scripture comes from someone's own interpretation. For no prophecy was ever produced by the will of man, but men spoke from God as they were carried along by the Holy Spirit. (2 Peter 1:19 ESV)

> "Only Jesus can produce generational change."

5

An Issue of Blood

"Hands up! Don't shoot!" became a cry of protest against police brutality years before the incident involving my son. The slogan circled around the debate of whether Michael Brown from Ferguson, Missouri, had his hands up or not when shot by police. The message indicated that a posture of surrender should offer protection.

The fallacy of that way of thinking is that surrender is not merely a gesture; it goes far beyond the action of hands raised—it rests deeply in a heart change. Committing a crime and then throwing your hands up is not a true surrender. It may be surrender by the world's standards, but it is a far cry from what Christ calls us to do.

My journey of surrender was a long one, but when I learned and truly began to understand God's Word through the power of His Holy Spirit, everything changed. As I go through the process of surrendering, I am learning who I am in Christ, and this is a powerful realization. To be claimed as the daughter of the King of Kings is an adoption unlike any other. There is power in this heavenly heritage.

What if every person knew the power of surrendering? What if every police officer or other person, black or white or any skin tone, knew who they were in Jesus Christ? What if every man, woman, and child, in any walk of life, knew who they were in Jesus Christ? Would this bring about change? Absolutely.

If people were to read the Word—truly read it, study it, believe in it, and grow in it, praying and fasting to know God's will—it would change everything. Some people would rather not read the Word, and as a result, they are bound by fear and the ways of the world. When we abide in the Word, that spirit of fear can no longer touch us. Racial discrimination would no longer mold us and take us captive. White supremacy would be no longer. Black supremacy would be a thing of the past.

What if we all genuinely understood that the Word of God is talking to us as individuals? If we did, there would not have been the cases of Michael Brown, Sandra Bland, George Floyd, Rodney King, and so many more. There would not have been a situation with Laquisha Booker and my son, Jacob Blake. These names wouldn't be in the media if our world surrendered to Jesus.

We mourn and grieve the tragic occurrences in life without seeking the deep roots of the only change that will make a difference. Would surrender to God produce real heart change? Yes. There would be no more school shootings, no more homelessness, and no more senseless violence. If the world lived for Christ, love would reign.

How can this be when imperfection dwells in each one of us? Even with surrender, does a world devoid of evil exist? That perfect world is coming. Jesus is coming, so why wait? Let us put on the whole armor of God. Let us not conform to this world but be transformed by the renewing of our minds. The politicians can't do it. New laws cannot do it. More police training cannot do it. We should know that by now. It is not the color of our skin or what colors we wear to work—it is the spirit we choose. Do we choose life, or do we choose death?

As a black woman, I have seen how we in the black community often hold ourselves captive. I understand what our group has been through, but we are not the only ones who have faced hardship and oppression. Historically, many people groups have suffered greatly and worked to repair the destruction of oppression. We are not the only ones. This is not stated to mitigate the horrific nature of the evil and vile slave trade. There is no excuse for what occurred. However, we can't keep dwelling on the pain that the masters did—the pain that systemic racism has given us or the ways it has hindered or held us back in our lives. We seek to blame this for all our problems without pinpointing the current roots in our own lives.

We have to examine the issue of blood, not just in the black community, but also in each and every household here in America and worldwide.

Nobody can force you to mistreat your blood relatives, the people you grew up with in your household. If your mother, father, sisters, and brothers are not loving, affirming, protecting, and providing for you, then how does that play into things? That cannot be blamed on racism. It is a matter of blood. It's an issue of the heart that only God Himself can fix.

I've often had this vision of being bloodied and bruised from the pains and the hurt of my life—by what happened to my son and what happened before my son was even a seed inside me. My bloodline afflicted scars on me long before the world did.

Generational sorrow and sin were flowing through the blood that I was born into. Maybe others can relate. Close family members don't always treat each other with respect. We often don't even treat ourselves with dignity and justice, so how can we treat others correctly if we have not learned how to respect ourselves?

In the Bible, the book of Luke tells a story of a woman with an issue of blood. She had been hemorrhaging for twelve years. She had tried all the ways that the world presented her for healing. She had spent all her earnings on physicians and cures, yet she still bled. However, one day as Jesus passed by her, she reached out her hand to grasp the hem of His garment. Immediately, power left Him and flowed into her, bringing instant healing. She had long searched for other solutions and failed, yet when she grasped for Christ, she was forever restored.

We need to figure out what's inside our hearts and reach for the hem of Jesus. I'm not talking about healing a medical disease. I'm talking about deep-seated heart disease. I'm talking about bloodline curses, where generations have tried to manufacture ideas of healing but have failed miserably. Our society is broken, and we have tried many solutions to fix our problems. But all solutions have failed except Jesus. Like the woman with the issue of blood, we need to reach out to Jesus, grasping Him to heal us. Only He can heal our broken hearts, broken families, broken dreams, and generational curses. Only Jesus can produce generational change.

We must acknowledge that we can't heal ourselves and that we need to surrender, yielding to God's purpose for our lives and wills. As other people label me, I am a black woman, but my identity is not in the color of my skin. My relationship with Christ is what defines me. When I surrender to His will, my heart changes, and so does the way that I see the world.

If we want justice as a society, we need it from God. His is the only justice that will change our lives personally and the entire human race. So what does surrender to God produce? We need to stop being bound by our skin and instead be shaped by deep compassion for each other. A heart of empathy is a gift from God, and we all desperately need it. I pray often for the compassion of Christ because I need it. It takes great strength to understand what others who may have hurt us are going through and to forgive or pray for them. This power goes far beyond the depths of our sin. The power to truly forgive and release the offense of another to the Lord is nearly impossible if not for the grace of God.

God forgives us for everything that we have done. He doesn't mention it. He doesn't bring it up again or weaponize it against us. He throws it as far as the East is from the West. When God forgives us, He is so gracious that, in Him, our sin is no more. This is true forgiveness.

We are not Jesus, but He does transform us. However, sometimes the process is a slow one. It takes time for us to come to a place of repentance and surrender, but we have to be willing to devote ourselves to that. Every day, we must give up the things that hurt us or our children and surrender them to the Lord. We have to raise our hands in the surrender of prayer and praise as we work to truly forgive.

As a nation, we have to learn to heal and forgive. We have to forgive those of our own blood who have caused us generational pain, and we have to forgive those who have drawn blood from us through systemic injustice. This doesn't mean that we allow abusive behavior against us to continue. We must have boundaries to protect our homes and our hearts, but within those boundaries, we also have to forgive by releasing others of any debt they owe us.

If it sounds like I am some sort of expert on surrender and forgiveness, I am not. In fact, they have been my greatest struggle and they continue to be. However, I know the difference between how things turn out when I do things my way, which is a path of pain, and the contrasting outcomes when I walk in God's will, which is a path of supernatural, all-encompassing peace. The protection of that path of peace is a place that I never want to leave, and the only way I find myself there is when I surrender to God's will.

I am definitely a work in progress. I struggle against surrender every day. I also struggle with forgiveness. I often think that I have forgiven when I really have just suppressed my feelings of anger and resentment. It is only when I examine my heart that I recognize this and ask God to work to make me new in Him.

Where I am lacking, God is working it out. He is cleansing me from any unforgiveness so that healing can come. When the healing comes, restoration from a relationship with Jesus accompanies that as well.

When receiving the gift of salvation, we are given a blood transfusion. We have the blood of Jesus inside us just as the Holy Spirit dwells within us. This blood transfusion makes us new. Our blood is washed clean from the inside out, and our perspective begins to shift from a worldly view to a Kingdom perspective.

As forgiveness fills our broken hearts, we move to a place of power through prayer. The Bible instructs us to love those persecuting us and to pray for our enemies. It is very hard to pray for people we view as enemies, but once we forgive them and are given hearts of compassion, we can extend that empathy to others. Without forgiveness, there is no hope for healing. As a culture, we can't move forward if we believe everyone else owes us something. We have to wipe the slate clean and start from a renewed vantage point. We must turn our hearts to God and learn to walk in His ways, or we will continue to see violence, oppression, and destruction.

> *As Jesus went, the people pressed around him. And there was a woman who had had a discharge of blood for twelve years, and though she had spent all her living on physicians, she could not be healed by anyone. She came up behind him and touched*

An Issue of Blood

the fringe of his garment, and immediately her discharge of blood ceased. And Jesus said, "Who was it that touched me?" When all denied it, Peter said, "Master, the crowds surround you and are pressing in on you!" But Jesus said, "Someone touched me, for I perceive that power has gone out from me." And when the woman saw that she was not hidden, she came trembling, and falling down before him declared in the presence of all the people why she had touched him, and how she had been immediately healed. And he said to her, "Daughter, your faith has made you well; go in peace." (Luke 8:42b–48 ESV)

"Prayer is a powerful connector of God's will in heaven to be done here on earth."

6

Pain Has a Purpose

A song by Mary Mary says, *"Take the shackles off my feet so I can dance; I just want to praise you."* I felt that song reverberate through my soul the second day that I saw Jacob in the hospital. The first time I saw him, he had been cuffed and shackled, remaining in police custody. That day, the shackles had been removed from his feet, but a police officer remained standing sentry in the stark hospital ICU room.

After some brief conversation about how he was feeling, I readied myself to pray with Jacob. Everyone always looks for ways to help in a crisis while they overlook the most powerful weapon in a spiritual fight or fight for someone's life—prayer. I wanted to ensure my child was covered in as much prayer as possible, so I prepared to pray with him. Bowing my head, Jacob stopped me, "Wait, Mom." His eyes moved toward the place where the police officer stood.

"Do you want to pray with us?" asked Jacob.

"Sure," responded the officer.

By Jacob's bedside, the three of us held hands and gathered in a poignant moment of prayer together. This was powerful. I didn't prompt Jacob to ask the officer to join us; he did it on his own. Those skeptical of faith may shrug this off and say, "That isn't significant. He was on a lot of painkillers and probably didn't know what he was doing." However, sometimes medication can act as a truth serum of sorts, and the truth was, meds or no meds, that was Jacob's heart. He may not always make the right decisions, but that is neither here nor there. The sheer fact that Jacob had just been shot up by a police officer, and yet he reached out to hold hands with an officer in prayer, was powerful. That moment will forever be written on my heart.

Prayer is a powerful connector of God's will in heaven to be done here on earth. This moment reflected that as sides that others thought should be opposing were instead uniting in prayer. They weren't warring with each other; they were joining to pray for healing. This is what God desires.

After the incident, I had a lot of questions. Why did this happen to my son? Why did this happen to my family? Why was this tragedy occurring in my life? There were a lot of thoughts swirling about the "why," but from the very beginning, God assured me that this attack by Satan on my family would not be without purpose. God would use it for His glory. And why not me? God had been preparing me my whole life to live in a Kingdom perspective instead of being bound by popular public points of view. I was ready to represent Christ however I could in this or elsewhere.

In my past, my life had been bound by pain, but now my shackles were off. I could see God's purpose through the pain because God and I had walked this road many times before, and this knowledge changed everything.

I didn't always feel this way. For most of my life, I felt shackled by pain, guilt, and shame. I distinctly remember walking through a family gathering when I was a young girl. As I made my way around family members, all I could think was, "Why? Why, God? Why am I even here?"

As I grew older, the bondage of painful memories and sin-filled secrets held me in a place of pain. The memories of shadows in the night entering my bedroom and touching me as no little girl should ever be touched, an innocence broken by things that should never be shown or taught, the pain of domestic violence and of fingers gripped in strangulation around my neck as my back was pressed painfully against a wall, the vile violation of a rapist's ravaging—these were traumas that terrorized me in a vicious stranglehold of shame and pain. I didn't yet realize that the shame of those events should rest on the perpetrators and not on me, and this lack of understanding victimized me again and again.

Then there were the many ways I added to the pain, amplifying it with drugs or alcohol, mostly in my teens, instead of drowning it out as I longed to do. My hurting heart lashed out. My pain poured over others whenever anything bad happened to me. It didn't matter if I were at home or at work; if something upset me, I would cuss and cry, rant angrily, and hold grudges. If I felt that an injustice had occurred, I would strike back by complaining to person after person about what had been done, growing angrier and angrier. I consumed my pain until it poisoned me and those around me. I knew this wasn't what God wanted me to do, but I did it anyway.

As a little girl, my siblings teased me, and I responded by trying out a torrent of four-letter words. My cursing made my siblings laugh louder, humiliating me. I learned to listen to the way that they cursed and practiced repeating the hate-filled words in the mirror until I became fluent in them. My language was laced with profanity that I used as a weapon wherever I went.

By the age of twelve or thirteen, I was already experimenting with cigarettes and alcohol. Soon I added marijuana to that mix, occasionally sampling other drugs with my siblings, and later with friends. I was on a quest to fit into a world that I was not made to belong to. I didn't understand that God had created me to be set apart. Instead, I longed to belong to something that only offered brokenness.

I stopped drinking, found out that I was pregnant when I was 18, and my marijuana use fell away too. Cigarettes, however, were my addiction. When I cleaned up from drinking and drugs, I substituted shopping as a vice. Somehow, I thought that if I just made enough money or bought nice things, it would take all my pain away. It never did. It just left me broke and broken. It never fulfilled the pull of my heart for something more. I needed to be delivered of these dependencies and behaviors, but I couldn't do it on my own strength.

Even in this time of brokenness, I would go to church and read God's Word, but my vision was so clouded by the pain of life that I couldn't accept that God had anything better for me. In my immaturity, I wrongly figured that the Bible didn't apply to me. It intrigued me and inspired me, yet I held it at an arm's distance, denying that there was purpose in it for me. Sure, I loved church and the spiritual high of praise and worship, but I was under such a heavy bondage of pain, confusion, and rebellion that I couldn't truly see and hear all that God had for me.

I understood that as we go through life, we experience a lot of pain living in a world overflowing with sin. I could see that pain was a common experience—I just couldn't understand why it had to occur and why I had to go through it. Everyone processes experiences differently, and for me, I just had to know why there was so much pain. I wanted to understand it and make sense of it. I prayed and asked the Holy Spirit to help me understand. I was led to read the book of Job in my Bible. This is a powerful story that raises many questions about the purpose of pain and suffering. My questions on this subject seemed endless, so reading Scripture that addressed the things I was wrestling with was encouraging.

The book tells the story of a man named Job, who was known for his righteousness and wealth. One day, his life was turned upside down as he experienced a series of calamities, including the loss of his children, his wealth, and his health. Job's friends and even his wife encouraged him to curse God and die, but Job remained steadfast in his faith.

Job's friends assumed that Job was suffering punishment for some hidden sin, and they urged him to confess and repent. However, Job was adamant that he was innocent and that his suffering was not a result of any wrongdoing on his part.

I knew that although much of my pain was due to no fault of my own, I was experiencing other pain that I had brought on myself through sinful actions. I had to repent of these sins.

Job, however, was righteous, yet God allowed him to suffer. Why was this, and how was this fair? The book of Job shows that pain and suffering could have a deeper, more mysterious purpose beyond punishment or retribution. God Himself allowed Job to suffer, and in the end, Job was not given a clear explanation for why he had to endure such pain. Instead, Job was challenged to recognize his own limitations and to trust in the wisdom and sovereignty of God.

Ultimately, the book of Job showed me that pain and suffering could serve to test, refine, and deepen my faith, among other things. I often wondered how God allowed me to be molested and to suffer through that as an innocent child. Job's story reminded me that even when I don't understand the reasons for my pain, I can still trust in the goodness and wisdom of God. Through my pain and struggles, I learned to depend on God more fully and grow in compassion and empathy for others who suffer. Job's story reminded me to trust God in all things, knowing that my pain was not in vain and that He had a purpose in each and every hardship. I could see this if I looked for it. I knew God could use even the most horrible experiences for His glory, yet I struggled to personalize this. How? How could God use my ratchet self for His good?

Over time, I began to sort through the various scenes of my life and to see God working. I knew that I had been foolish many times with my decisions and my life. I also knew that a lot of people viewed me as the worst of the worst. How can I be used for God's glory? God certainly wants to use us, but we often let shame disqualify us. Shame is a weapon Satan uses to keep us from doing what God calls us to do, and this weapon was definitely working against me.

As I began to sort through my thoughts, one of the leaders at my church, who was my mentor, suggested that I get involved in women's ministry. I thought, *What? Me? No, I can't do that. I have had too much pain in my life to minister.* It took me a while to recognize that serving others who also had pain and hurt was exactly where God wanted me to be.

What if I stepped out of my comfort zone and left shame behind, only to get rejected if I ministered? This was always my fear, but I realized I would rather be rejected for serving God than accepted for serving only myself. I wondered how anything good could come out of me. It wasn't that I was a horrible person; it was that my heart had been horribly broken and damaged. I didn't see how God could use that, but He did. He allowed me to minister to others with similar experiences, and as He healed my brokenness, He also used me to bring healing to others.

I was still learning that God will use our pain and that no trial will be wasted. In fact, the Bible is full of stories of God using a lot of very imperfect people for His glory. Most of the people in the Bible screwed up, messed up, had pain, and were imperfect, but God still valued them and used their stories for good. There is powerful assurance in that.

Pain Has a Purpose

I felt that my own story was embarrassing, shameful, and often sad. How could God use me? However, looking back at everything that happened, I could see how God brought me through it all. This was undeniable. I wanted to blame God for all the bad that happened, but when I examined my heart, I could clearly see that while my experiences had been hard, God had been protecting me in so many ways, even when I hadn't realized it.

I am glad that I learned this long before the event that happened with Jacob because when I asked, *Why us?* it became clear. The circumstances of his shooting were horrific, but Jacob was still alive, and it was clear that in the midst of the mess, God was working for good. Not only that, but this time, my eyes were open, and I knew the promise that this pain would also produce hope.

How would God use this? At that moment, I wasn't sure, but I knew that He would, and I saw glimpses of this all around me. Praying with the police officer was a glimmer of this promise. Speaking from a Kingdom perspective at the press conference was another glimmer that God was working. The outpouring of love and support from the community was a beautiful thing. Even the difficult things, such as God refining my heart for forgiveness, were developing for good. God was working just as He always does. Pain does not prevent Him from the power of His promise.

Praise be to the God and Father of our Lord Jesus Christ, the Father of compassion and the God of all comfort, who comforts us in all our troubles, so that we can comfort those in any trouble with the comfort we ourselves receive from God. For just as we share abundantly in the sufferings of Christ, so also our comfort abounds through Christ. If we are distressed, it is for your comfort and salvation; if we are comforted, it is for your comfort, which produces in you patient endurance of the same sufferings we suffer. And our hope for you is firm, because we know that just as you share in our sufferings, so also you share in our comfort. (2 Corinthians 1:3–7 NIV)

> "God was not the author of our pain or the destruction that occurred to Jacob's body, but He would use it to write a story of victory."

7

Love Your Children Before You Have Them

"Love your children before you have them." I heard this statement as a teenager, possibly in my home economics class or maybe in some other class, but for whatever reason, I have remembered it ever since. *How can you love your children before you have them?* I wondered. At that time, I didn't even know if I even wanted children or would have them, so it seemed impossible to think about loving them. It sounded like the silliest idea in the world to me.

No matter which way I turned it around in my mind, loving my children before I had them just didn't seem to make sense. As a teenage girl who was very troubled, this phrase seemed absolutely ridiculous to me. It wasn't until I became a mother of three that I started to understand the truth of this statement. In the Bible, Jeremiah 1:5a says, "I knew you before I formed you in your mother's womb. Before you were born, I set you apart." This is profound. If God knew us before we were born, then being the God of love, He loved us. Before we were even conceived, God loved us unconditionally, which is unfathomable. This is so powerful. God loved us, even knowing all of the ways that we would sin, hurt ourselves and others, mess things up, and get things wrong. His love is without conditions or qualifications. It just is. It is a love so deep and endless that it is astonishing.

God's Word also tells us that God has plans for us. Before we were born, He loved us and had plans for us. *What were his plans for me and for my precious children? What were His plans for Jacob lying there all shot up in a hospital bed?* I wasn't sure, but I knew that God's love for Jacob was greater than I could ever comprehend. Although I hadn't been able to grasp the concept of loving a child before you even knew that he would be born. God knew, and He loved us all. I was confident that no matter what happened, the Lord would work plans for His good and the glory of His purpose. God was not the author of our pain or the destruction that occurred to Jacob's body, but He would use it to write a story of victory.

At one point, while we were in the hospital, a surgeon came to speak to Jacob and me. He explained to us that he had been attending to Jacob since he arrived at the hospital by helicopter. The surgeon expressed his sincere condolences. He discussed damage to Jacob's body—the spinal injuries, his liver and kidney damage, and the place where his stomach had been struck. Jacob had lost his entire colon and most of his intestines, but God was merciful to the point of him not needing a colostomy bag. His bladder was damaged as well.

The surgeon explained to us that Jacob would require additional surgery to place brackets in his back to stabilize his vertebrae. If Jacob did not have the surgery, he would end up paralyzed from the neck down, and his life expectancy would be very short. If he did have the surgery, he would be in tormenting pain for the rest of his life. We had to make the decision between two immensely difficult outcomes.

Jacob was awake for the conversation, and despite the extremely heavy medications, he was able to process what the surgeon was saying. The surgeon emphasized that a decision had to be made then because it was likely that the surgery would one day become critical, and Jacob would have to be rushed into the operating room without time to deliberate. He cautioned us both that now was the time to think things through and to weigh and pray about the options.

I told Jacob to make the decision and expressed that I would support him in whatever he chose to do. It was important to me that I didn't push my own perspective on what would be a life-changing decision for him in either direction. Jacob chose to have the surgery. It turned out to be beneficial that this discussion took place because, as the surgeon had warned, the surgery was later carried out with no forewarning. The next day when I went to see Jacob, I was told by the hospital staff that he was already in surgery again. They hadn't been able to call me before he was rushed in.

That day dragged by excruciatingly slowly as I waited to hear the outcome of his surgery. It lasted somewhere between twelve and sixteen hours, all of which seemed an agonizing wait. I sat and prayed, pouring my heart out to God as I waited for an update.

When Jacob was finally wheeled out of surgery and I was allowed to see him, I sat at his bedside and watched him. His body was a road map of tubes, wires, scars, and stitches, marking a pain-filled path to wherever God would eventually lead him.

As grateful as I was that my boy was alive, it was hard to see him in that condition. While he was battling to survive, I was battling in my own way with feelings of failure. I loved my child so much, but I also felt that I had let him down. I thought, *What did I miss? What could I have done differently as a mother—not just with Jacob, but with my other children too? Was I a horrible mother? Had I let my children down too many times? Did I not talk to them enough? Did I not punish them enough?* I was quite certain that I had. God is a perfect Father, but I know for sure that I was not a perfect mother. However, I did the best that I could in the circumstances that I was in, and I had to trust that God would cover the rest.

That head knowledge does not always convert to heart knowledge, and I began to gauge my parenting with a hyper-critical eye.

I thought back to a time when Jacob was often ditching his high school classes. It happened enough that it drew the attention of the school administration, and an officer came to my job to address it. I was furious. I was struggling as a single mom to provide for my three kids. I asked the officer, "Have you ever tried to contact his dad to ask why he's not helping? No? But you come to my job when I am the only source of income for my children." I placed so much blame on everybody around me, but I also heaped blame on myself. It was difficult to face the reality that many factors contributed to what had happened in the past and what was occurring now.

The truth was that in the same way in which I viewed my children with love in spite of their mistakes, I needed to view myself in a more loving and grace-filled perspective. I made many mistakes as a parent, but I also raised three wonderful children, mostly on my own. Thankfully, my mom was also there to help me as I raised them, and I thank God for that because I couldn't have gone to work or school without her. My mom wasn't perfect either. We were both broken people trying to raise the next generation while still in a broken place. I didn't have any business trying to raise three children in that place, but somehow God made a way when there was no way. He poured grace over grace on me, my mom, and my children as we struggled our way through this sin-filled world.

These thoughts wrestled with me as I sat with Jacob. Thoughts of mistakes made and failures that occurred warred with worries about Jacob's future. I wished so badly that he had just come home and started over again instead of staying with Laquisha in Wisconsin. I wished that he had found a better way to share custody and moved back with me or with his sisters. If he had started over in a safer situation, maybe this wouldn't have happened. I wanted to go back in time and rearrange all the pieces of his life to come up with a different outcome, but there was no going back. I could only love my son the best I could within this situation.

I may not have loved my children before I had them, but I loved them all fiercely now, and I wanted their best. I had to acknowledge that God loved Jacob with an even greater love than I could ever imagine and wanted for his best too. My struggle with surrendering to God didn't change in this situation. I knew that in all things, I had to trust that Jesus had a plan to redeem, and I had to hope that Jacob would surrender to God's will as well.

I knew that I had failed many times as a parent. I was broken and human and needed discipline for myself. Oh, how I wished that I had applied God's loving authority to my life before I had my children. It would have been a wonderful thing to parent from a place of healing instead of brokenness.

I knew that even in my brokenness, I had done some things right. I disciplined my children the best way I could. I taught them right from wrong. I paid their bills, fed them, clothed them, housed them, and nurtured them. I taught them about Jesus and took them to church. As I spiritually matured, I hoped that my kids would be able to recognize the difference in me and know that it was a good thing. I wanted them to see the contrast between when I had parented in brokenness versus parenting from a place of healing—that they would see that I was able to love them more with God's love as I grew in Him.

My broken love for my children couldn't change their futures, but I knew that God's healing love could. If God could bring me to a place of healing and surrender, He could bring Jacob to this same place. He could also bring our country to restoration.

No matter what mistakes I made in the past or what I would do going forward, I knew that, ultimately (like us all), Jacob was responsible for his own actions. His behavior would reveal whether he grasped this chance at a new beginning in Christ and if he recognized that he had been saved from death for a reason. I surrendered him to God even as I covered him in prayer. I stood in prayer for my son, for Laquisha, for the Blake family, for the police officer, and for those in turmoil and rioting. I prayed that their hearts would change and be healed in Christ.

To truly love as Jesus loves, we have to pray for everyone. We need to pray for our police officers. We need to pray for the gangbangers and drug dealers. We need to pray for those who hurt us, betray us, or persecute us. God desires that we pray for everyone—not just those who look like us or think like us. We need to pray that the unsaved will be saved. We also must pray that the Lord will create in each of us a clean heart and a right spirit, as He forgives us of our sins.

We need to stop the killings. We need to stop the shootings. We need to stop the hatred. We can't feed it. We have to turn from it. We need to stop promoting division, and we must see each other through the loving eyes of God. We need to recognize that differences enhance our society instead of dividing it. We need to love people before we know them and value them for who God made them to be.

God is an incredible Creator who loved us before we were born and created each of us in a brilliantly unique way. We are not all black and not all white. We do not all act the same way or think the same way. Imagine if God made only one kind of flower or one type of food. That would be boring.

When a flower blossoms, our first thought is never that we kill or harm all other flowers around it so that only one type of flower can shine in its beauty. This would be ridiculous. There's so much beauty in a field arrayed with diverse wildflowers, each growing in the loveliness of its unique shape and colors. Yet, it seems that societally we set out to damage those who we see as different. We push a narrative that divides instead of recognizing beauty and strength in each other.

We need to pray for unity. We need to pray that, like the surgeon who worked so hard to save Jacob's life, God would do a heart surgery of sorts on us—that He would replace our hardened hearts with hearts that love and value others. This is His desire for us. He is a healer, and our hearts need healing.

> *And I will give you a new heart, and a new spirit I will put within you. And I will remove the heart of stone from your flesh and give you a heart of flesh. (Ezekiel 36:26 ESV)*

> "Before we address systemic issues, we have to address what is in our own hearts."

8

Hearts That Heal

As Jacob lay in the hospital, the wounds of our nation were growing deeper. The rioting in Kenosha was ramping up, and the city was erupting in violence and looting. The governor had declared a state of emergency in Wisconsin, and the White House authorized 2,000 National Guard troops to be deployed. A deep political and societal chasm had formed, and the hurt of what had occurred was pushing the two sides further apart.

The media continued to promote the divide, as did lawyers, talking heads, and the Blake family. There seemed to be no middle ground. No bridge existed between different perspectives. Hurt was turning into hate, and hate was an inferno that consumed everything surrounding it. The buildings and broken windows bashed by the looters could be repaired, but how would the hurting hearts find healing? How could there be reconciliation or restoration when cries for retaliation were echoing around the city?

The answer was in the one place where people didn't want to look. People wanted answers in action, but they needed answers from above. They needed to cry out to Jesus. He knows every heartache, every sin, and every injustice. He knows pain more than anyone because when He died on the cross, He took all of our pain, shame, and brokenness. Jesus was beaten, rejected, spit on, mocked, and crucified, yet He did that for us. He died and rose again so that we could have new life in Him—and we desperately need new life.

No one can look at what happened in Kenosha and say that the world's way of doing things is working. It is not, so why do we keep returning to it? Why don't we try another way?

When we are sick in our bodies, where do we go? When our hearts are hurting, who is the one who can heal us? We need to run into the arms of our Creator and know that the very God who has numbered the hairs on our heads has the power to heal our hearts and our land.

I can't imagine how devastating it would have been had I lost my son to that shooting. And I cannot for one second tell any mother or father who has lost a son or daughter to violence, in any shape, how to feel. However, if you are that parent, I can tell you that I know who can get you through it. I know who can heal you. Whether or not the person who did the wrong is punished, only God can heal you. You can take that pain and give it to Him so he can use it for His glory. He doesn't want us to live our lives with pain, anger, unforgiveness, strife, and malice. Those things will destroy us and everyone around us.

We can't just check into church every once in a while and expect life to be different. God's Word instructs us to pray without ceasing. I sin and make mistakes every day. I have to change. I have to pray and ask God to take my heart and make it clean. I have to pray that I will not embrace the world's anger, but that He will renew a right Spirit within me. Those evil spirits that God has pushed out will come back if I leave the door open to them. I can't do that. I can't step away from God, or I will fall back. I need to push forward, falling on my knees in prayer and then walking step by step toward God. Our country needs to do the same.

To be transparent, I have fallen back many times. I did that earlier in my walk with the Lord. When my kids were young, I joined a church and got involved in as many activities as possible. I was on the usher team and the prayer team. I was at church as often as I could be—usually three to four times a week. I was so active with the church that my daughter Megan told me I had churched her out. That may have been true, but I was there.

I had jumped in with both feet, but then I stepped back into the world. I still went to church, but when

I wasn't there, I was living in my old rebellious ways. Shame was pulling me back to the world, but I knew that the shackles needed to break. I had been down this road before, so I kept going to church. I knew that God was a chain breaker and that I needed to follow His path.

And because of my rebellious spirit, it took longer than it should have. But God broke those chains, and He can do it for you. God will chase you and pursue you endlessly. You are chosen by Him, and He wants to take you in as an adopted son or daughter of the King of Kings. He wants to show you how His perfect love drives out all fear and brings you peace—an overwhelming, supernatural peace.

I know that God does this because He did it for me. He rescued me from my ratchet brokenness and rebuilt me as beautiful in Him. He turned my rebellious and hardened heart into a heart filled with love and compassion. Without God, I can do nothing. Every time I have tried to live without God, it has caused more pain and hurt, but when I was transformed in Him, healing came, bringing peace, comfort, and joy in all circumstances.

Recently, I was picking up my grandsons from school, and the oldest asked a question about God's creation. We looked around and noted the birds soaring above us, the trees growing in their towering strength, and the radiant warmth of the sun—all of these things were made by our Creator. All the materials that we use to create houses, playgrounds, schools, roads, bridges—these are all made by God too. God gave mankind the wisdom and knowledge to learn how to create and build them. Many of these things have been used for incredible good, but the flip side to that is that some can be used for great evil.

God has created everything for good, yet because of human hardness of heart, so many things can be manipulated or used for destruction. We have seen this throughout history, and we see this particularly with race. God made people in beautiful different shades and appearances. An artistic Creator, this design was not accidental or a mistake. We have to see this. We have to see each other with love, compassion, and purpose. When we recognize this, we can make room for healing to occur.

Healing also comes from the recognition of brokenness. When my son was shot, people everywhere erupted in anger. They might not have been personally affected, but it triggered something hurting inside of them. I understand this. Before the Lord began healing me, if I was in a dangerous situation, my mind would somewhat black out—not in a faint, but just a mental absence. It was as if I were there but not there. I could still function, yet I was also frozen. I would be present, but my mind would be zoned out. You could be talking directly to me and I wouldn't hear a thing. I know that this was a reaction triggered by the pain and distrust due to being molested as a child. This caused me to develop this defense as a form of protection.

However, instead of addressing it and trying to heal, as one observer put it, "When things get tough, you have the tendency to put your head in a hole like an ostrich." At first, I became defensive when I heard this, but when I sat with it, I recognized that it was true. I couldn't control or prevent the pain of the trauma that had occurred to me, but it was my responsibility to heal. I had to face the truth that the hurt that I had gone through was causing a visceral, physical reaction that, if unaddressed, would continue to worsen. I knew that God had allowed me this physical reaction as a protection from trauma, but I also understood that He was the answer to my healing. I had to allow my Creator to heal the underlying issues that were causing the system failure in the first place.

When an injustice occurs, it makes sense that it would trigger a response deep inside of us. We should respond to injustice. However, our response should never be a lashing out in an eye-for-an-eye reaction. We need to heal the root cause of our pain. We need to seek our Creator and ask Him to cut to the heart of what hurts us.

Systemic racism deeply bothers me as it should hurt the heart of everyone. I know that it grieves the heart of God. Burying my head in the sand and pretending that it doesn't exist would be foolish. It bothers me, but if I let myself be consumed with anger over it, it will ultimately consume me. Instead of viewing myself as a victim of systemic racism, I choose to believe that I am who God says that I am. I don't let any other human being tell me my worth or rely on another person to make me feel worthy or whole. I have learned that no one can define me but Jesus Christ Himself. My prayer for my black and brown brothers and sisters and everyone else is that we would no longer live in past history—that our present will bring each person to understand that God says that we are fearfully and wonderfully made and God has plans for our good.

If we allow the oppression of systemic racism to turn our hearts to hate, this will only serve to nurture more hate. This hate will not create reconciliation; it will continue to divide and multiply oppression. We cannot allow ourselves to be consumed by hatred. We need to look in the mirror and take our God-given gift of salvation, redemption, healing, and renewal of mind, body, soul, and spirit. We need to repent and put on the mind of Christ.

We have to allow God to heal us. We have to turn our hearts to Him. Before we address systemic issues, we have to address what is in our own hearts. Even as I am writing this, I know that people will say, "That is not enough! We need to do more than repent, pray, and heal. We need to take action." Maybe this is true, but the most powerful action that we can take is appealing to our Creator and letting Him reign as King.

With our broken and hard hearts, we think we know all the answers. We think we know how to fix problems, but we don't, or they would be fixed already. We have tried it our way. We need to try it God's way.

In the Bible, the Israelites petitioned the prophet Samuel to ask God for a king to rule over them. They rejected the loving and righteous rule of God and demanded that a human king rule instead. They desired something outside of the will of God, and He allowed it, and the people suffered the consequences of their choices:

> *Then all the elders of Israel gathered together and came to Samuel at Ramah and said to him, "Behold, you are old and your sons do not walk in your ways. Now appoint for us a king to judge us like all the nations." But the thing displeased Samuel when they said, "Give us a king to judge us." And Samuel prayed to the Lord. And the Lord said to Samuel, "Obey the voice of the people in all that they say to you, for they have not rejected you, but they have rejected me from being king over them. According to all the deeds that they have done, from the day I brought them up out of Egypt even to this day, forsaking me and serving other gods, so they are also doing to you. Now*

then, obey their voice; only you shall solemnly warn them and show them the ways of the king who shall reign over them."

So Samuel told all the words of the Lord to the people who were asking for a king from him. He said, "These will be the ways of the king who will reign over you: he will take your sons and appoint them to his chariots and to be his horsemen and to run before his chariots. And he will appoint for himself commanders of thousands and commanders of fifties, and some to plow his ground and to reap his harvest, and to make his implements of war and the equipment of his chariots. He will take your daughters to be perfumers and cooks and bakers. He will take the best of your fields and vineyards and olive orchards and give them to his servants. He will take the tenth of your grain and of your vineyards and give it to his officers and to his servants. He will take your male servants and female servants and the best of your young men and your donkeys, and put them to his work. He will take the tenth of your flocks, and you shall be his slaves. And in that day you will cry out because of your king, whom you have chosen for yourselves, but the Lord will not answer you in that day."

But the people refused to obey the voice of Samuel. And they said, "No! But there shall be a king over us, that we also may be like all the nations, and that our king may judge us and go out before us and fight our battles." And when Samuel had heard all the words of the people, he repeated them in the ears of the Lord. And the Lord said to Samuel, "Obey their voice and make them a king." Samuel then said to the men of Israel, "Go every man to his city." (1 Samuel 8:4–22 ESV)

If we turn our hearts away from God and continue to seek solutions and retribution on our own, He may give us our requests. He may allow us to live in our own will instead of His, and just like the Israelites, we will discover that this is a hurting, oppressive, and destructive place to be. Unless we change our hearts, we will be stuck in this seemingly never-ending cycle of systemic racism, violence, and harm.

The only solution for healing and change is surrendering our hearts to Jesus Christ and seeing Him bring His peace, His comfort, His healing, and His restoration.

If my people, which are called by my name, shall humble themselves, and pray, and seek my face, and turn from their wicked ways; then will I hear from heaven, and will forgive their sin, and will heal their land. (2 Chronicles 7:14 ESV)

"Hard-hearted pride is not just a black or white problem. Pride is a human broken heart condition."

9

A Humbled Heart

On September 4, 2020, Jacob was required to make a court appearance from his hospital bed at Froedtert Hospital. In the peak of COVID culture, court hearings were occurring more frequently online, and with Jacob in the hospital, it seemed the only option for him was to appear virtually in court.

The lawyers asked me to go out and buy Jacob a dress shirt and tie for the appearance. The problem was that Jacob was still in excruciating pain, and his back was incredibly tender, so we couldn't dress him as you would a healthy individual. It was impossible to put a shirt around his pain-filled back.

We had to prop Jacob up in his hospital bed like a living mannequin, cutting the shirt down the back. We arranged everything to look as if he were wearing a full shirt and hoped it wasn't obvious that it was open behind him. We buttoned the front of the light blue shirt as if he were wearing it fully, and we neatly tied his yellow tie.

Jacob pled "not guilty" to three charges that had been made against him in July: third-degree sexual assault, criminal trespass, and disorderly conduct. A bond of $10,000 was set for him, and the court instructed him that he was not to go to Laquisha's house, obtain a weapon, or leave Wisconsin except for medical treatment.

A few days after the incident when Jacob had been shot, Laquisha pulled me aside at the hotel to talk. Prior to everything unraveling with the shooting, I did not know that Jacob had been under a restraining order. That confused me because Jacob and Laquisha were still spending time together, co-parenting, and talking as usual. From my vantage point, I could see no indication that their relationship was altered in a way that would require a restraining order.

That being said; however, Jacob is an adult and often does his own thing. So many times, I didn't know about something he had done until after it occurred. In fact, two or three weeks before the shooting happened, Jacob had been in Las Vegas hanging out with some friends, and I didn't know about that at all until after he got back. It wasn't necessarily my business, but it surprised me that he didn't mention it until later. In this case, though, with the restraining order, neither Jacob nor Laquisha had said anything to me about it.

A Humbled Heart

A day or two before Laquisha asked to talk, I ran into her sister in front of the hotel. She asked me, "Aren't you mad at Laquisha?"

I was utterly oblivious to what she was talking about, and I was confused, I replied, "I don't think that I need to be." We were interrupted before I could ask further questions and find out what she was talking about.

When I was able to sit and talk with Laquisha, she said, "I have to talk to the police, and I don't know what to say."

"What do you mean you don't know what to say?" I asked. "You tell the truth. Whatever that truth is, you tell it. You tell the truth about you. You tell the truth about Jacob. You tell the truth about everything."

Laquisha cried a bit, saying, "Mama, I want you to know Jacob never raped me. We got into it and were both drunk, and you know, I called the police, and they tried to get me to say that he raped me. He didn't rape me."

According to her, when they later went to the police station, they found out that it was in the police report that he raped her. Laquisha and Jacob went to the station, and she told them that part wasn't true. She asked them to take it out of the report. She signed a paper and was told, "Don't worry about it."

I wasn't sure what to make of this revelation except to say that as a victim of rape myself, it is always in my heart to hear from the victim and learn the truth. I love my son, but in a situation like this, I needed to hear from the victim and not the accused about whether or not the allegation was the truth. Victims need to be heard and believed without bias. In this case, I needed to separate myself from the fact that Jacob was my son and listen openly to what she was saying. When Laquisha told me that Jacob didn't rape her, I believed her.

That knowledge took some burden off my heart but didn't alleviate it completely. Those two should have never been together. Their clinging to something dead and toxic almost killed Jacob. This call to the police wasn't the first domestic call leading up to this. It was one in a series of calls that most often took place when Laquisha was drunk, Jacob was drunk, or they were drunk together.

Jacob called me on one occasion, saying, "Mom, Laquisha's drunk. She's trying to leave, and I've got her keys. I don't want her to leave because she is drunk, and she is calling the police on me."

That time the police came and talked with them and left. When Jacob called me back, he told me, "It's okay. She's asleep now. She's not going to leave. She's going to sleep it off."

A Humbled Heart

I was so frustrated by their constant cycle of destruction. I kept thinking: This is not fair to anyone involved, not even the police. Ya'll may not like or even understand my saying this, but it is true. We have to protect them from repeat calls like this. This is not fair to the children. They shouldn't be stuck on this merry-go-round from hell forever. Mandatory measures should be put in place to keep this from recurring. If there are multiple domestic calls, let's protect the police and the children. Let's put mandatory counseling measures in place before a couple can be back together after domestic calls. If two grown-ups can't figure out on their own that someone will get hurt if they keep getting together, something must be done to prevent the cycle and protect innocent people from repeatedly getting drawn into a dangerous and volatile situation.

I was tired of this cycle and was distraught that it had led to the terrible outcome. Just as we had dressed up Jacob in a nice shirt and tie to make him appear better than the physical condition that he was in, often we try to dress up our sin and minimize it to be less than it is. We try to pretend our perspective, no matter how broken, is one of righteousness. We clothe ourselves in prideful opinion without seeing that pride will always bring a fall. We try to dress respectably and feign perfection when we are living in a pride-filled spirit that has to be humbled, or it will continue to harm. I wish Jacob and Laquisha had humbled themselves enough to separate before the situation escalated. I hope that our country will humble itself before we experience the wrath of God's judgment.

In the Old Testament of the Bible, Nebuchadnezzar, the King of Babylon, witnessed God working mightily over and over again. Yet, he pridefully claimed all glory for himself, stripping honor from God that belongs only to Him. Daniel 4:29–33 (ESV) states:

> *All this came upon King Nebuchadnezzar. At the end of twelve months he was walking on the roof of the royal palace of Babylon, and the king answered and said, "Is not this great Babylon, which I have built by my mighty power as a royal residence and for the glory of my majesty?" While the words were still in the king's mouth, there fell a voice from heaven, "O King Nebuchadnezzar, to you it is spoken: The kingdom has departed from you, and you shall be driven from among men, and your dwelling shall be with the beasts of the field. And you shall be made to eat grass like an ox, and seven periods of time shall pass over you, until you know that the Most High rules the kingdom of men and gives it to whom he will." Immediately the word was fulfilled against Nebuchadnezzar. He was driven from among men and ate grass like an ox, and his body was wet with the dew of heaven till his hair grew as long as eagles' feathers, and his nails were like birds' claws.*

A Humbled Heart

As soon as King Nebuchadnezzar pridefully took the glory for all that God had made and given him, God removed him of his power and radically humbled him. He was punished severely for his pride, and for seven years, Nebuchadnezzar was driven out of his kingdom and lived like a wild animal in the wilderness.

When Nebuchadnezzar was finally restored, it was with a deeply humbled heart, and instead of self-praise and pride, his praise belonged to the Lord (Daniel 4:34–37 ESV):

At the end of the days I, Nebuchadnezzar, lifted my eyes to heaven, and my reason returned to me, and I blessed the Most High, and praised and honored him who lives forever, for his dominion is an everlasting dominion, and his kingdom endures from generation to generation; all the inhabitants of the earth are accounted as nothing, and he does according to his will among the host of heaven and among the inhabitants of the earth; and none can stay his hand or say to him, "What have you done?"

At the same time my reason returned to me, and for the glory of my kingdom, my majesty and splendor returned to me. My counselors and my lords sought me, and I was established in my kingdom, and still more greatness was added to me. Now I, Nebuchadnezzar, praise and extol and honor the King of heaven, for all his works are right and his ways are just; and those who walk in pride he is able to humble.

As humans, we are often are filled with pride like Nebuchadnezzar's. We think that we know everything and that everyone should bow down to our opinions. We hate and believe every lie we hear about others, further stoking the fires of that hate. We choose sides and erect a wall of pride that obscures the truth that is found in the humility of loving others and gently listening to the wisdom, experience, and perspectives of those different from us.

Hard-hearted pride is not just a black or white problem. Pride is a human broken heart condition. Christians, we aren't exempt. We often think we hold a moral high ground based on our own thoughts when Christ calls us to humility. We believe that we are somehow better than others when we are called to serve. If we don't change ourselves to have hearts of humility, how can we expect change in others who don't know Christ? We can't point to Him if we are exalting ourselves or our own way of thinking. We must remain humble, seek the truth of God's words, hear the hurt of others, and serve those surrounding us.

We have to know the heart of the Lord to be able to walk in His ways. We do this by reading the Word of God, studying it, and meditating on it. Our worldly accolades don't accredit us to God; He sees our hearts. He doesn't judge us by skin color, educational level, professional accomplishments, or annual income. We all have to face God at judgment, and that judgment is coming. In our pride, we think that we know what the Lord wants, but what He usually requires of us is just the opposite.

Isaiah 55:8 says, "For my thoughts are not your thoughts, neither are your ways my ways, declares the Lord." The world's priorities and values are very different from God's. This is true for almost any area of life—from racial disparities to anger to hatred to murder to walking with pride. The Lord hates these attitudes of evil. We may not understand or agree with each person's lifestyle, but we are still called to treat everyone with love, kindness, and respect.

It takes humility to pray for those who hate and hurt us. It takes a hunger for the Lord to turn from things that feed our pride and anger and to nourish attitudes of gentleness, understanding, and loving boundaries. The vanity of humanity and worship of our own ways will lead to destruction if we don't humble ourselves and turn to the one who is the true Way.

We must stop worrying about how we look on the outside and focus on renewing our hearts. We have to learn that without Christ, we can do nothing.

If my people who are called by my name humble themselves, and pray and seek my face and turn from their wicked ways, then I will hear from heaven and will forgive their sin and heal their land. (2 Chronicles 7:14 ESV)

"We don't have to be enough because Jesus is already more than enough."

10

A Love without Fear

While Jacob was in the hospital, security was incredibly tight. Visitation was already limited due to fears of spreading the SARS-CoV-2 virus, but the growing violence in Kenosha had enhanced security concerns, especially around Jacob. Everyone was nervous about what would happen next as things remained at a breaking point.

During Jacob's hospital stay, I received a call from hospital security saying they needed to see me. I nervously walked through the long hospital hallways, wondering what awaited me in the security offices. There I found five to ten brightly wrapped packages that they said were for Jacob's children. Someone had dropped them off, saying they were from a church, but they did not leave a church name or contact information. Security asked if I was expecting packages. I replied that I was not. So many threats were going around at that point that security had become concerned about these packages that had no specific purpose or identifiable origin. They strongly cautioned me not to accept the gifts, and I agreed. It was a scary time, and I was worried about accepting strange packages. I gave security permission to dispose of them however they wanted to before returning to Jacob's room to continue watching over him.

That time period in the hospital was so unpredictable. The COVID-19 pandemic had already tilted us far from the realm of normalcy, but now we were dealing with security concerns, stressful family dynamics, media pressure, and challenges to Jacob's health. Entities on either side were quick to dox both my son and Officer Sheskey, which put both families in danger as personal information and home addresses surfaced for public access.

Media inquiries were coming in every day. Reporters were eager to capture Jacob's point of view on camera. However, given the physical pain that he was in, paired with high doses of pain meds, Jacob was not in camera-worthy shape. Instead of being plagued by the media's thirst for more fodder to stoke their headlines, he needed to rest and recover. It wasn't just the media that was swarming. Strangers claiming to represent Jacob or the family were collecting money or donations in his name—much of which he never received.

Due to many of these concerns, combined with COVID-19 restrictions, the only people with regular access to Jacob were me, his father, and his lawyers. Yet, somehow someone gained access to Jacob in the hospital without my knowledge or permission and interviewed him from his hospital bed.

The release of the interview angered me. I was horrified to see the video splashed across media outlets everywhere. I was furious because it felt like exploitation. Those of us caring for Jacob knew that he was in no shape to be speaking publicly, yet somehow the release of this video had been orchestrated. He was on powerful pain medications at that time and barely remembered making the video, and he didn't remember authorizing it.

It seemed that there were two camps of people—those who genuinely cared about Jacob's recovery and well-being contrasted by those who cared about creating and fueling a divisive campaign of outrage and agenda.

Those who operated with love and care deeply ministered to our family during that trying time. The hospital staff was exceptional, and the bedside manner of almost everyone we encountered was overflowing with kindness and compassion. God ensured we were ministered to in a time of pain and grief.

On the flip side, many voices speaking out the loudest to the media were not the same people showing consistent care and concern for Jacob. One exception was a lawyer who diligently visited Jacob nearly every day in the hospital. Some days he would arrive before even I did. He quickly became my favorite lawyer because it was clear that he viewed Jacob as a person and not as a platform for media attention. This was meaningful and made a difference in the whirlwind of our circumstances.

The reality was that we were in a seemingly impossible situation. Even with as much progress as he was making in the hospital, Jacob was still in bad shape and was in a state of constant pain. His muscles would spasm painfully, and the feeling that he did retain made his legs feel as if they were being shredded in a wood chipper. Paralyzed from the waist down, we knew Jacob's recovery would be a lifelong process, and I tried to mentally prepare myself for that.

As Jacob's mother, I knew I would become his primary caregiver. I struggled to wrap my mind around how I could provide constant care while I worked full-time to support myself. The hospital seemed a fearful place. More unknowns were facing us than knowns. The safety concerns, Jacob's health concerns, and my concerns for the future were working to bring me from a place of supernatural peace to a place of fear, and I didn't like that. However, as usual, I sought the Lord for reassurance.

If I am afraid, God's answer is, "Fear not, because I am with you; the Lord, the God of Jacob, will be with you wherever you go." If I say, "Lord, I'm weak," He says, "My strength will make you strong." If I think,

"Lord, I don't know how," He says, "My Holy Spirit will lead you." If I believe that I'm not good enough, "My grace is sufficient," says the Lord. If I think, "No one will listen to me because of my past," Jesus shows me His own genealogy full of imperfect people whose familial line God still used to raise His perfect Son.

We don't have to be enough because Jesus is already more than enough. Sometimes the weight of everything seems too heavy for me, and I feel like giving up. I have grown enough in my faith that in times like this, I know that I need to seek God's Word. There Jesus reminds me, "My yoke is easy, and my burden is light." When I am sad or overwhelmed, I immerse myself in the Word of God, and the joy of the Lord gives me strength.

God constantly reminds me that His ways are so very different from ours. It is like an upside-down kingdom compared to this world that we know. When Jesus came to this earth, those around Him expected Him to use His power and might to overcome the ruling government at that time. Jesus, the King of Kings, did the opposite. He became a servant, washing the feet of those who followed Him.

When I think no one will listen to me, the Lord reminds me, "It will be My words that you're speaking and not your own." If I say, "I am unqualified because of the depth of my sin," Jesus says, "My blood covers your sins." If I think, "I am not qualified to share Your message; I don't even have a college education," Jesus says, "I give you My wisdom. It is not the wisdom of the world, but wisdom from God above." If I demand reparations for the wrong things done to me, Jesus tells me, "Revenge is the Lord's. Cast your cares on Me." If I cry in despair throughout the night, God's Word assures me, "I will take away your tears." If I say that I am unworthy, God says, "You were worth the blood of My Son, Jesus Christ."

If I say, "I don't know how," God's Word reminds me that I was predestined to speak to the nations before I was born. If I ask, "What about my job, God? I have to work," God assures me, "I am the supplier of your needs." Every question that I take to the Lord is met with an answer from His Word. Every doubt that I have is replaced with His truth. His confidence covers every fear that I have. Many people in my life have failed, harmed, or exploited me, but not God. He is always good. He holds me in every circumstance and daily renews my strength with His faithfulness and great mercy.

I am probably more imperfect than almost anyone on earth, yet God uses me. I find this mind-boggling, but I am so grateful that the God of all creation would work through me. He works through all those that give their lives to Him.

Knowing that God works through me makes me endlessly humble and grateful. And as I experience

God's mercy and grace, how can I not show mercy and grace to others? God has taught me so much. Even through the process of this book, He has been showing me new things as He molds me and makes me examine my own heart to grow and be more like His. Admittedly, sometimes it's hard for me to open God's Word and learn more because sometimes I'm tired. I simply don't feel like doing anything but just zone out. But then I have to ask Him to give me the desire to seek Him. I pray, "Give me ears so that I may hear, eyes that I may see, and a heart that I may receive. Lord, I want to pay attention to details like Noah, to have faith like Abraham, to be courageous like Moses, to praise You like David, and to love and forgive like Your Son. Lord, I need you." Whenever I pray that prayer, He is always faithful to honor it as He desires that I have a renewed heart—a heart like His.

As a culture and country, we need to have a heart change. We must call on the Lord for mercy, forgiveness, revival, and reconciliation. The world has made us slaves to things we hold up as idols. We make gods out of celebrities, technology, and even ideologies. We have made gods out of fear, anger, hurt, and intimidation. We make gods out of clinging to sin that hurts and harms. The world teaches us that anything can become a god, yet the Bible tells us there is no other God besides the one true God. We need to repent and call on the Lord to be saved. This is the only way to heal our hurting hearts.

For God so loved the world, that he gave his only Son, that whoever believes in him should not perish but have eternal life. (John 3:16 ESV)

> "I desire that you see Jesus in everything I have written and you are overcome with a desire to know Him more."

Epilogue

Full Surrender

It has been nearly three years since Jacob was shot. I would love to tie up this book with a story about how our life has changed for good since the incident. However, the reality is that our everyday life is filled with fairly brutal challenges as I work to care for my son. Yet, even amid the harsh realities of life, God continues to make a way where there has been no way.

It hasn't been easy. I remain my son's primary caregiver, and it is very difficult. I'm still watching my son's body deteriorate, and on some levels, he is deteriorating mentally and emotionally as well. Chronic pain is a vicious experience. Even watching all the stages he is going through, I still don't fully understand it as I am not in his mind or body. I am just an observer of something incredibly complicated.

The family dynamics are consistently challenging. There have been a lot of disagreements and differences of opinion. It can be exhausting, yet I continue to see God working. He is refining and rebuilding all of us to have hearts more like His. It is an arduous process, though it is one that bears fruit.

From the date of the shooting until February 2021, I wasn't able to work due to caring for Jacob full-time. I gradually returned to work, yet caring for Jacob and my aging mother made full-time work impossible. It has been a difficult journey, yet I trust in God's provision.

Sometimes I see fruit in Jacob's life, and sometimes I see only hurt. A year ago, in an interview with TMZ, Jacob said, "I understand that people usually don't survive after getting shot seven times like I got shot, you know…. I am a firm believer in God. And before this, I didn't believe in Jesus Christ, but after this, yes, I surely do. And ain't nothing gonna change it. Nobody can tell me anything different because I know what happened to my body and every bullet except for the two that hit my arm. That's five bullets that should have killed me, but they didn't."

The fact that God used this tragic shooting to draw Jacob to unwavering faith in the Lord is a miracle, and I trust that God will continue to work to shape and refine his life. The fact that Jacob was able to forgive the police officer and allow God to give him care and compassion for Officer Sheskey's family is also a beautiful work that could be done only by God.

Many of you probably opened this book seeking a salacious view into the background details of what happened in this tragic situation, but I hope that something else met you as the Holy Spirit spoke through my words. I desire that you see Jesus in everything I have written and you are overcome with a desire to know Him more.

A parable in Matthew 13 tells of a farmer planting seeds. Some seeds fell on a path and were quickly eaten by birds. Some seeds fell on rocky ground where they couldn't grow deep roots, and the sun scorched them until they withered and died. Other seeds fell among thorns where they grew up and were quickly choked to death. Some seeds fell on good soil and were nurtured and grew in abundance for generations.

The Word of God is like this. It touches many people, but they must nurture in their hearts to be like good soil to allow growth and development. I often pray that God makes my heart like good soil so His Word will continue to spring up in me. I pray that Jacob's heart becomes like good soil and that God's merciful intervention forever changes his life. I pray that you, as you read this book, hear God's voice and respond. Allow what He is nurturing in you to grow root and not be choked and die. I pray that you hear God speaking to you and respond in surrender.

Suppose you are reading this and wondering what you need to do to experience God's salvation. It is very simple. You must come to the knowledge that you can do nothing to earn God's grace or favor because it is a gift freely given when God sent His only Son to die on the cross for your sins. On the cross, Jesus took all the punishment for your sin on Himself. A sacrifice was made so that you can become a son or daughter of the living God. You only need to repent and ask Him to fill your heart to experience a heart change like none other.

Pray with me: Dear Jesus; I need Your help. I know I am a sinner, but I believe You died on the cross as payment for my sins and rose from the grave in victory. Please forgive me for all my sins and help me to turn my back on those thoughts and behaviors. Please come into my heart and change me from the inside out. Please help me to have a heart like Yours. Please teach me how to trust and love in Your perfect love. I surrender to You. In Jesus' name, I ask this. Amen!

> *Because, if you confess with your mouth that Jesus is Lord and believe in your heart that God raised him from the dead, you will be saved. (Romans 10:9 ESV)*

Printed in the USA
CPSIA information can be obtained
at www.ICGtesting.com
LVHW041535271023
762201LV00014B/1860